A Woman With a Man Beside Her

Stories for the Better Half

Dan Madson

Skrive Publications
Miramar Beach, FL

Printed in the U.S.A.

ISBN #: 978-1-952037-00-9

SKRIVE PUBLICATIONS

Miramar Beach, FL 32550

www.skrivepublications.com

TABLE OF CONTENTS

DEDICATION

This book, like the others, is dedicated to my wife. Her success in the Mary Kay world has allowed me the opportunity to do things I never thought possible.

A Letter to Husbands

Dear Husbands,

When Dan told me he was planning to write a book for Mary Kay husbands, I was not very enthusiastic. In fact, my reaction was similar to his reaction 20 years ago when I told him that I was going to start my own business. He persisted in his belief that a book like this would be valuable and after thinking about it for a while, I realized he might be right.

When a woman starts a Mary Kay business and has support from her husband from the beginning, she has a much greater chance of succeeding. Her journey will also be a lot more fun.

Over the years, I have seen a lot of women who have what it takes to be successful in this business—a strong work ethic, endless drive and energy, along with belief in the company and the products. They start out eager and enthusiastic with the chance to be great Mary Kay Independent Consultants, Sales Directors, or even National Sales Directors. When faced with negative pressure at home, however, many of these women have become discouraged. Some have quit.

I'll never forget Dan's reaction when I told him that I was going to become a Mary Kay Beauty Consultant. "That's fine," he said, "Just don't expect any help from me."

Not to be deterred by his noncommittal response, I thought to myself, "Wonderful! I have his blessing."

Dan became supportive after my very first week of sales. It made me feel so much better to know that he was behind my efforts. I wanted to do well not just for myself but for him and for our children. Knowing that he understood and supported my goals was very important to me, especially in the beginning.

If I could offer you any advice, I would tell you to *always* be encouraging. When your wife faces disappointments and frustrations, pat her on the back—high up—like Mary Kay used to say. Give her the freedom to succeed. Allow your wife to treat her business *like* a business and you and your family will benefit.

Love and belief,

Lisa Madson

INTRODUCTION

I wrote this book primarily for men and organized it in a way that men can appreciate. That's not to say that women won't find the book enjoyable. It's just that most women don't watch *SPORTSCENTER* on a regular basis. I think most men would agree that *SPORTSCENTER* is one of the few shows on television worth watching. Depending on their schedules, men can get their daily sports fix in the morning, midafternoon, early evening, or at bedtime.

The show begins with little more than its signature theme song — DA-na-NA, NA-na-NA! Then, without wasting any time, the announcer begins to review the top sports stories of the day. Each story is accompanied by highlights, of course. The format of the show has not varied much in 20 years. Loosely organized yet tightly scripted, *SPORTSCENTER* jumps from topic to topic faster than Paris Hilton changes boyfriends.

The first two stories might be about the NFL. From there the announcer segues into a story about the winner of the week's PGA Tour event. After that it's college football and then news from the World Series followed by a recap of the latest NASCAR race. The highlight of each day's show? The Top Ten Plays of the Day. Rim-rattling dunks, long birdie putts, touchdown catches, fiery crashes, and tape-measure home runs. If you happen to tune in during the middle of the show, it doesn't matter. You know that something of importance in the sports world will be coming up shortly.

Each chapter in this book has a simple, one-word title and is a story in itself. The chapters are not organized alphabetically or chronologically. If you sit down to read and can only finish one chapter, that's OK. You will learn something about Mary Kay Cosmetics, the company, or about your wife's personal business in each chapter. I would suggest keeping the book in one of the libraries in your home.

We have five libraries in our house, and on the back of each stool you can find a diverse collection of reading material from *Sports Illustrated* to *Triathlete* to *People* or the latest books by John Grisham, Stephen Hunter, or Malcolm McDowell.

This is not a "how-to" book. It's more like a "Why not me?" or "Why not us?" book. Its purpose is to help you grow as a Better Half. Mary Kay used to say that a woman with a man behind her is a woman and a half. It's true! If you take an interest in your wife's business and learn ways to support her, there's a good chance she will prosper and you will benefit.

I have been a Mary Kay husband for nearly 20 years and have experienced just about everything a Mary Kay husband can go through. My hope for you is that after reading this book, you will better understand the importance of dreaming, planning, and working together. Without further explanation, DA-na-NA, NA-na-NA!

Chapter 1 BEGINNINGS

I had heard of Mary Kay Cosmetics before my wife decided to join the company. I knew that the company's trademark color was Pepto-Bismol pink and that its top people drove Cadillacs of the same color. That was about it. I didn't know anything about Mary Kay the woman until my fourth year of teaching.

That summer, in preparation for a creative writing session in my seventh grade classroom, I picked up a book called *Creative Encounters with Creative People.* The book featured a variety of well-known inventors, entertainers, and entrepreneurs—people like Thomas Edison, Henry Ford, Walt Disney, and Oprah Winfrey. Toward the end of the book there was a section on Mary Kay Ash. I started reading the biography that explained how Mary Kay began her company. I was intrigued by her unusual business philosophy of "God first, family second, and career third."

As a teacher in a Christian school and father of two young children, I was impressed. Early in the school year when I started using the book, one of the suggested activities at the end of the lesson about Mary Kay Ash was to invite a Mary Kay Independent Beauty Consultant or Sales Director into my classroom to explain her business. I had brought other parents into my classroom to talk about their careers, so I thought it would be interesting to find somebody that sold Mary Kay and invite her to speak to my students.

On the night I sat down at our kitchen table to organize my lesson plans for the next day, I reached for the phone book. My initial thought, foolish as it seems now, was to see if Mary Kay herself would be able to come and speak to my kids. When that search proved fruitless, I turned to the Cosmetics section of the Yellow Pages and found six listing for Mary Kay

Independent Sales Directors. I discovered that one of the women listed in the phone book lived three blocks from our house. I called her immediately, explained who I was, and asked if she would be willing to come into my classroom and talk about her business. She seemed happy to oblige, and we set a date for her to speak to my students the following week.

When that day arrived, the Mary Kay lady pulled into our school parking lot in her pink car. She was dressed in a navy blue business suit and carried herself with poise and confidence. She spoke to my students for 30 minutes and told them how she had started her business, how she built a sales unit, how she earned money, what type of teaching she was responsible for, and the like. She did a great job, and at the end of her presentation she asked if there were any questions. Hands shot up immediately. "Have you ever met Mary Kay?" "Why did Mary Kay choose pink for her company's color?" How much money do you make?" "Can we have some free stuff?"

My class enjoyed the woman's presentation, and I was impressed. After she left, the kids gathered around the window of my classroom to get one last look at her as she strode across the parking lot, disappeared into her pink trophy on wheels, and drove away. When I got home from school that day, I told Lisa about my experience with the Mary Kay Independent Sales Director who lived up the street.

—

3

Lisa didn't say much. It wasn't until later that I learned why. What I didn't know is that this woman had bumped into my wife two weeks earlier as Lisa had been making photocopies for her boss at a local print shop. The woman walked into the establishment and smiled at Lisa, who was standing near the door. Lisa smiled back as she undoubtedly would have to anybody who smiled at her first. The woman introduced herself and said, "I think you would be great doing what I do."

"Oh, no thank you," Lisa said. "But I do know who you are."

"You do?"

"You're my Mary Kay Beauty Consultant."

"I am?"

Lisa bought so little makeup that her consultant didn't even know who she was.

"What's your name?" she asked.

"Lisa Madson."

"I'm going to remember that."

Lisa is embarrassed now to admit that she thought to herself, "You go right ahead. I would *never* do something like that."

I'm sure the woman would have agreed to speak to my students even if she had not previously met my wife. But perhaps she wanted to make a favorable impression on Lisa by doing me a favor—I'm not sure. In any case, that chance encounter and my classroom invitation set the table for a relationship that would change both Lisa's life and mine.

Not too long afterward, Lisa ran out of the foundation she had been using for years. She called her beauty consultant to order some new products. After the consultant took the order she asked Lisa a very simple question. "Could I please come over and talk to you for one hour?"

Thinking it might be the only way to get rid of her, Lisa reluctantly agreed.

When I got home from school that evening, Lisa greeted me as I came in from the garage. "Guess what?" she said excitedly.

"What?" I said. An array of thoughts flashed through my head before she could answer. Had she cracked up the car? Burned dinner? Dropped Rachel down the basement steps?

"I'm becoming a Mary Kay independent beauty consultant!"

I paused briefly. I knew that Lisa had planned to meet with her consultant that morning, and I knew she was going to tell her no if asked to sell the product. When she surprised me by declaring that she had joined the company, I was not very enthusiastic. Then again, I usually didn't get too excited about most things. I responded in a calm but dubious tone of voice. "Well, I suppose that's OK," I said. "Just don't expect any help from me."

> **Had somebody told us then that those six boxes of product would launch what would one day become a multi-million dollar business, I think we both would have laughed!**

I was a busy man! I had a heavy workload at school that included full days in the classroom, before-school supervision, recess duty, and lunch duty. I was also the athletic director and president of the parent-teacher organization, and I coached five sports. In addition to those duties, I officiated high school basketball during the winter and baseball during the spring to earn a little extra money. We had two little kids at the time, ages four-and-a-half and three, and I didn't see how it was possible for me to help with anything else.

Lisa must have interpreted my apathetic reaction as tacit approval for her new venture because she went skipping back into the kitchen to take care of dinner. Later that evening I started asking questions, but I had only one thought in mind.

"What's this company all about?" *Translation: How much is this going to cost us?* "Do you have to go to some sort of training? *Translation: How much is this going to cost us?* "Are you required to get some inventory? *Translation: How much is this going to cost us?* "How could you let her talk you into something like this?" **Translation:** *How much is this going to cost us?* Finally I asked the question uppermost in my mind. "How much is this going to cost us?" **Translation:** *Are you crazy?*

Lisa seemed awfully excited and appeared to be confident in her ability to go into business on short notice and without any experience, so I grudgingly decided to tag along just to see what would happen. After all, even guys like Carnegie and Rockefeller had to start somewhere.

Not only had Lisa signed a contract to become a Mary Kay independent beauty consultant, she had also decided to get an inventory so that she had some product on hand to sell. Her starter kit arrived a couple of days later. A few days after that the UPS man dropped off six boxes of products on our front stoop, and Lisa was in business.

At this point I have to admit that I was getting somewhat excited about her new venture. Even though I didn't have any business experience myself, I'm a capitalist at heart and was interested in the concept of a person (my wife, in this case) owning her own business. I even helped her arrange an office in the basement of our first small home, which we rented from Lisa's parents. I salvaged an old steel desk from school, dismantled it, carried it piece by piece down the basement steps, and reassembled it next to the oil tank – a rusted green monstrosity – that sat against the wall in the utility room. It's contents were used to fire the ancient furnace in an adjacent room. To the wall next to the furnace, the previous owner of our house had nailed pegboard on which to hang his tools. I replaced the tool hangers with small trays and hooks and helped Lisa unpack her inventory.

I carefully arranged all the boxes by size, color, and product description. I hung eyebrow pencils in order from darkest to lightest. I stacked boxes from smallest to largest. Lisa didn't seem too concerned about my attention to detail. She simply said, "Don't worry if everything isn't stacked straight. The idea is to sell it all right away."

I would not, however, be dissuaded from carefully arranging everything in perfect order. When all six boxes were empty we stood back to look at her new store. If somebody had told us then that those six boxes of product would launch what would one day become a multimillion-dollar business, I think we both would have laughed!

SUGGESTION: Establish an office for your wife and keep the business in that part of the house.

Chapter 2 PRIZES

My wife is not motivated by prizes. At least that's what she'll tell you if you ask her. Yet I'd be willing to bet that she would be happy to show you the beautiful jewelry she has earned from Mary Kay or tell you about the wonderful trips we've enjoyed to exotic destinations all over the world. Me? I've always been motivated by prizes. My second grade Sunday school teacher was the first person who ever offered me a prize to achieve a goal. I remember it vividly. It was a multicolored pen, big as a cigar, that had 12 different colors of ink inside. By clicking a particular button at the top of the pen, you could send any one of those colored points out the other end. In order to earn that fantastic prize, I think I had to recite some Bible passages or hymn verses. I don't really remember. All I knew was that if I accomplished what my teacher wanted me to, I would get that pen.

When I got my first paper route during the summer between my fourth and fifth grade years, I had the chance to earn prizes if I could sell extra subscriptions to the *Minneapolis Star-Tribune*. I'll never forget the one prize I earned that summer. It was an army-green hatchet with a nifty leather holder that I could slide right onto my belt. As soon as I got it I sharpened it to a razor finish on my neighbor's grinder and promptly started hacking away at anything that I felt needed to be chopped into small pieces. Unfortunately, that prize caused me some pain and suffering.

> **The prize that cemented the company's reputation for variety and generosity in my mind, however, was a John Deere riding lawn mower.**

One afternoon I stopped at Al's Garage to buy a can of Shasta cherry cola. When I tried to open the tab, it broke off, leaving the soda inside inaccessible to a very thirsty boy. I carried the can home, set it on the counter, carefully eyed the stubborn top, and unsheathed my trusty hatchet. Holding the can with my left hand, I swung the bottom edge of the blade down toward the top of the can in order to enlarge the opening. The blade bounced off the can and sliced into my left hand. It opened a gaping cut from the bottom of my index finger across to the base of my thumb.

Blood gushed from the wound, and I caught a glimpse of the white bone of my knuckles. Before the pain even began to register in my brain, I realized I was in trouble. I dropped the can and the hatchet, grabbed a clean white dish towel off the counter, and clamped it over my left hand. The blood quickly soaked through the towel and stained it a vivid crimson. Then it started to hurt.

I was the only one home and didn't know what to do, so I ran out the front door of our house and started screaming for help. My friend's mother, who lived across the street and happened to be a nurse, heard me and came running. When she saw the bloody towel that I had wrapped around my hand, she pulled it away to inspect my injury. When I saw her cringe, I became even more anxious.

She immediately bundled me into her car and drove me straight to the hospital. It turned out to be the first of many trips to the emergency room in my younger days. Despite the scars that hatchet left on my hand, I carried it around with me the rest of the summer and left some scars of my own on more than a few of my neighbors' trees.

When I learned that Lisa was eligible to earn prizes each quarter just for doing her business, I was more excited than she was. Every three months a prize brochure arrived in the mail. I would grab it and see if there was anything I thought she should select. Even though many of the prizes were appropriate only for women, I was surprised at the variety the company offered.

During her first few years as a Mary Kay Independent Beauty Consultant and later as a Sales Director, Lisa earned a plethora of prizes. There were telephones and tape recorders, big-screen televisions, silverware, computer equipment, a video recorder, and others too numerous to mention.

The prize that cemented the company's reputation for variety and generosity in my mind, however, was a John Deere riding lawn mower. It was a beauty! Even though our lawn wasn't big enough to justify the use of a rider, I still longed to have one. I pleaded with Lisa to choose it if she earned enough credits. As you might imagine, she wasn't personally enthused about choosing a lawn mower for a prize, so in my mind I wrote it off as a hopeless cause. I figured she would pick a more glamorous prize like a ruby ring or a new leather coat.

Early in September of that year the weather remained unseasonably hot. My classroom was like a sauna, and I remember coming home from school one day with the unappealing thought that my grass was still long enough to conceal small children and desperately needed mowing. I turned into the driveway and there it was. The GX-75 mower sat facing toward me from just inside the garage. The riding lawn mower that I had been coveting for six months had arrived and I still insist that it was smiling at me.

Sweating profusely, I strode into the house and barged right in on a gathering of five of Lisa's unit members who were there for a meeting. I got down on my knees in mock humiliation and said, "Thank you! Thank you! You are the BEST!" The girls around the table looked at me and then started laughing. Lisa explained to them what she had done, and I think they were as happy as I was.

I rode that faithful green machine back and forth in my yard for 10 years. My boys learned to ride it when they were old enough and took over the job of mowing the lawn. When the novelty of mowing wore off or they were too busy, I was always more than happy to hop aboard and cut the grass. It was, in my opinion, the best prize the company ever offered. After it was delivered, I never saw another prize brochure.

SUGGESTION: Ask your wife to show you the company's quarterly prize brochure.

Chapter 3 **C**ars

The main reason Lisa started her Mary Kay business was to earn extra money for Christmas in 1986. After she'd worked for a few months, her Sales Director told her that it was also possible for her to earn the use of a free company career car. Lisa tried to explain to me what she had to do in order to qualify for this reward. It seemed like a complicated process, and the only two words I could remember when she was done were *free* and *car*. From my experiences up to that point in my life, the word *free* had never been remotely connected with the word *car*.

Being the pragmatic person that I was, my response to Lisa's excitement was, "I'll believe it when I see it in the driveway."

When it comes to cars, nobody will ever confuse me with Jay Leno. I don't have a collection of fancy vehicles sitting in my garage. In fact, I didn't own my first car until after I got married.

When I was in high school, my father allowed me to drive any of his three cars. I remember all of them vividly. There was the gold Buick station wagon with wood-grained side panels, the canary-yellow Volkswagen Fastback with its engine in the trunk, and the pumpkin-orange 1972 Ford Pinto, notorious for its exploding rear gas tank.

Before my junior year in college my father sold me the Pinto for $50. He probably thought he was doing me a favor when, in the best-case scenario, he had saddled me with a recalcitrant means of transportation. In the worst-case scenario he had consigned me to a flaming death if I should get rear-ended.

In all fairness to the Ford Motor Company, that car did serve me well for one year, with a few small exceptions. The shock absorbers were shot. The transmission was temperamental. The tires were balding. The brakes were shaky. The heater didn't work very well. The radio was broken. The tail pipe had fallen off. And the driver's side door, which had never hung straight, was impossible to close. As soon as it was opened, it sagged under its own weight and

I had to lift it before slamming it shut.

One day in late fall, I returned home from school and tried to shut the driver's door. It wouldn't latch. I opened and closed it five or six times before I got frustrated. Finally in a fit of anger, I kicked the door shut as hard as I could. The latch finally caught, but the window shattered inward into a million tiny pieces. I left the car sitting in the driveway to suffer. The next morning I opened the door, scraped the heap of broken glass onto the floorboards, got in, and drove away.

As winter approached and the temperatures dropped, I dressed in a thick, hooded sweatshirt with a heavy coat on top of that. I tied the hood snugly around my head to keep out the cold since I had no intention of paying for a new driver's side window. I'm sure I turned a lot of heads that winter as I roared through campus. But I just looked straight ahead and pretended not to notice that the body of the car was nearly scraping the tires and the sound of the exhaust system was loud enough to damage eardrums for blocks. The only service I provided for that car was to fill it with gas and occasionally put a quart of oil in the crankcase when the engine light started flashing. At the end of the school year when the Pinto finally conked out and refused to start, my plan to drive it off the edge of a nearby quarry had to be changed. Instead, I called a local salvage company to come and pick it up. The junkman ended up giving me $25 for whatever could be salvaged, loaded the car onto the back of his flatbed truck, and hauled it away. With $25 in my pocket I felt as though I had gotten the better end of the deal. I never saw the Pinto again.

After Lisa and I got married, the first car we owned was called a Fiesta, another fine Ford product. About four feet long and three feet high, it was barely big enough for the two of us. Still, after Rachel was born, we managed to cram a car seat into the back, and the vehicle served us faithfully for five years. Today, I see car seats that are as big as that Fiesta.

The problem was that we both had jobs and when we each needed a car to go to work, one of us had to make a concession. I was teaching at the time, and my school was about two miles from our apartment. Since Lisa worked in another town, I didn't think it would be fair for her to have to ride her bike 45 miles to work, even though the thought of asking her crossed my mind. Consequently, on the days she had to work, I would ride my bike or take the city bus to school. Neither option was palatable.

After we moved into our first home and Lisa started her business with Mary Kay, we were still a one-car family. Granted, we had upgraded from our Fiesta to the much more luxurious Ford Tempo sans air conditioning, but we desperately needed a second car.

To help us out for a while, Lisa's parents loaned us the use

—

of Aunt Florence's LTD. Aunt Florence had been consigned to the old folk's home and had voluntarily relinquished her trusty green tank to her favorite niece, who in turned loaned it to her needy daughter and son-in-law. We understood that the use of this car was temporary. Since I was tired of biking to school in a suit and wingtips, I encouraged Lisa to keep working hard in order to earn the use of a Mary Kay career car.

At the time, the first car a Mary Kay Independent Beauty Consultant could earn was a red Oldsmobile Firenza. Lisa had posters of that car plastered all over her office and on the refrigerator in the kitchen. When we drove around town and saw a car that was similar, she would remark, "Hey, that's the car we're going to be driving!" She even taught our kids the words to the once-famous Mary Kay V.I.P. car song. I can still hear them chirping away in the backseat as we drove around. "Hey, look at me, I'm a V.I.P. girl, marching for Mary Kay!"

"I'll believe it when I see it in the driveway," I said. By now, those words had become a standing joke between the two of us. Her business was taking off and I was starting to believe that before too long a brand-new red Firenza might just be sitting in the driveway at 4805 Allis Avenue.

On October 31, 1987, one year after joining the company, Lisa earned her first company car. I tried to remain unemotional about it but, honestly, I was thrilled! After two

---

months she finally got a call from the Oldsmobile dealership telling us her car had been delivered and that we could pick it up the following day. Unfortunately, that night we were hit with a snowstorm that dumped 17 inches on the city. Many businesses, including the car dealership, closed in order to dig out, so we had to wait an entire extra day to pick up the new car. A few weeks earlier, Lisa had made me a promise. "Since you've been so helpful and supportive, I promise that you can drive it first."

Two days after the storm, we met at the car dealership after school. Lisa's sales director and her husband were there to greet us and help us celebrate. The kids were bundled up in their snowsuits, and they both held balloons that the receptionist had given them. I jumped right into the driver's seat, closed the door, and started exploring the buttons, ignoring the salesman as he tried to explain the features of the car. When I looked up, Lisa was standing outside the driver's door with a puzzled look on her face.

I rolled down the window. "You said I could drive it first!"

"I didn't think you'd actually take me up on it," she said.

"Come on. Hop in!" We caravanned home and parked the new ride in our garage. That night before bed, we both went out into the garage and sat in the car one more time. Had the roads been passable we probably would have tooled around the neighborhood for a while. Instead we just sat there and inhaled the new-car smell. Finally Lisa turned and looked at me.

"You'll believe it when you see it in the driveway, huh?" she said sarcastically.

"Did I say those words?"

"Yes, you said those words."

"I always knew you could do it!"

> **As a man, you might be thinking to yourself, "I would not be caught driving a pink car." To be perfectly honest, I thought the same thing until I had the opportunity to drive one. Trust me when I tell you that when your pink car comes, you'll be ready for it!**

Now that we were officially a two-car family, we returned Aunt Florence's LTD to its rightful owner and Lisa set her sights on her next goal—earning the famous pink Cadillac.

During her first year as a sales director, Lisa's unit had qualified for the pink Buick Century and shortly after that, the pink Cadillac. She decided to turn down the Buick and wait for the Cadillac instead.

The story goes that when Mary Kay wanted a special car to celebrate her company's achievements, she went to her Cadillac dealership to place an order. When the salesman asked her what color she wanted, Mary Kay told him to paint it pink. The salesman said, "Mary Kay, no! You can't have your car painted pink."

Mary Kay insisted. "Paint it pink." So they did. Since that time, the pink Cadillac has been the preeminent symbol of success in all of Mary Kay. General Motors, the company that produces the cars for Mary Kay, has copyrighted "Mary Kay Pink" as the color that is used exclusively for the fleet of Cadillacs driven by Sales Directors and National Sales Directors all over the country.

As a man, you might be thinking to yourself, "I would not be caught dead driving a pink car." To be perfectly honest, I thought the same thing until I had the opportunity to drive one. As Lisa's business grew and she worked her way toward new achievements, it became clear to me that she would be driving a pink Cadillac sooner rather than later. When that day came, I was more than ready.

First of all, I knew the pink Cadillac symbolized something special, and I was proud of what my wife had accomplished. In the years before Lisa joined Mary Kay I remember snickering every time I saw somebody driving a pink Cadillac. Despite my negative reaction, deep down I knew that the drivers of those cars had achieved something extraordinary.

Secondly, Cadillacs are wonderful cars. Until you've experienced the ride of a brand-new Cadillac, especially one that somebody else is paying for, you might not be convinced.

Mary Kay always referred to the pink Cadillac as a trophy on wheels. And it was. After Lisa earned her first pink Cadillac, I drove it every chance I could. More than once I was asked, "Do you actually like driving a pink car?"

"As a matter of fact, I do," I'd say. And then I'd typically add, "I wouldn't care if it was polka-dotted. It's free!"

The Career Car Program offered by the company remains a great avenue of income for Consultants and Sales Directors. As Lisa says to husbands whenever she speaks, "The first car your wife can earn is red. We'll *ease* you into pink." Trust me when I tell you that when your pink car comes, you'll be ready for it.

SUGGESTION: Ask your wife to explain the Mary Kay Career Car Program to you.

Chapter 4 HISTORY

The history that Lisa and I have with Mary Kay Cosmetics is not very different from that of thousands of others who have made the choice to go into business for themselves, set big goals, and then work hard to achieve them. None of it would have been possible except for the remarkable vision of Mary Kay Ash, the founder of the company. There are better books than mine to read if you desire a comprehensive understanding of Mary Kay's history. I would recommend *Mary Kay*, her best-selling autobiography, Mary Kay's *You Can Have It All*, or Jim Underwood's *More Than a Pink Cadillac*.

Mary Kay launched her company on Friday, September 13,

1963, an ominous date. With $5,000 she had saved after a 25-year career in direct sales and against the stern advice of her lawyer, Mary Kay decided to start her own cosmetics company. Her company would give women the chance to achieve many of the things that she had been denied during her career in a male-dominated sales company. I wonder if the conversation between Mary Kay and her lawyer sounded something like the following.

"Mary Kay, do you have any idea how many cosmetics companies went bankrupt last year alone?"

"Those stories don't matter. This will be my company, and my company will be different."

"You realize that you are putting your entire life's savings at risk, don't you?"

"This money is simply the seed that will grow into something great."

"Mary Kay, as your lawyer and financial advisor, my advice would be to liquidate your assets and get out while you can."

"I don't have a crystal ball and neither do you, but I know we can do it. We *have* to do it!"

The determination and can-do attitude that Mary Kay displayed throughout her life had their foundation in her childhood. Her father was often ill, and her mother worked long hours as the manager of a restaurant in Houston. Since

Mary Kay's brother and sister were grown and gone, the responsibility of caring for her father fell on her shoulders. Beginning at the age of seven, Mary Kay would come home from school, do her homework, and then cook and care for her invalid father. When she had questions, she called her mother on the telephone and asked what she should do. Her mother would patiently explain how to make potato soup or how to fix something that had broken.

Mary Kay didn't complain. She just did whatever needed to be done. And when faced with challenges that bewildered or scared her, she always remembered her mother saying "You can do it, honey." She undoubtedly heard those words thousands of times as a child and later repeated those same words to others just as many times. When Mary Kay looked you in the eye and said, "You can do it," you believed it could be done.

After retiring from her first career, Mary Kay decided to write down the things that she liked about the company she had worked for and the things she would change if she could run her own. After reviewing what she had written, she decided to take action and put her ideas into practice. With the help of her first husband and armed with a hide tanner's unusual recipe for a skin care formula, she drew up plans for her own cosmetics company. A month before she hoped to open for business, her husband died suddenly of a heart attack. Undaunted by this setback, Mary Kay made the decision to move forward.

Her 20-year-old son, Richard Rogers, quit his job with an insurance company to help her get started. On that fateful Friday in September of 1963, one month after her husband's funeral, the doors at Mary Kay Cosmetics opened for business with nine salespeople and with Richard as her financial advisor. Despite the overwhelming odds against her, Mary Kay knew that she had no choice but to succeed. And succeed she did!

I met Mary Kay for the first time in June of 1988. Lisa was a brand-new Independent Sales Director and was attending New-Director Training. I drove to Dallas with her and Kyle, our youngest child, who was three months old at the time. Kyle was still nursing and needed to be united with his

> **When Mary Kay looked you in the eye and said, "You can do it," you believed it could be done.**

mother periodically throughout each day. I spent most of my time at the Renaissance Hotel and would drive over to corporate headquarters every few hours to see Lisa. We didn't have enough money to eat at restaurants, so I bought a jar of peanut butter, a loaf of bread, and a dozen apples and subsisted on that simple fare the entire week.

On Tuesday afternoon of that week, as I was pushing Kyle

around in his stroller on the first floor of the company's headquarters, an elderly man wearing an official-looking badge greeted me. It turned out that he was employed by the company. His job was to guide tour groups through corporate headquarters. We struck up a conversation, and before I knew it he asked if I would like a quick tour of the building. I said "Sure." He showed me around and we eventually ended up in Mary Kay's office, where he allowed me sit behind her massive desk. When we returned to the first floor, I started walking toward the room where Lisa was meeting. Who should come walking toward me but Mary Kay herself, escorted by her personal bodyguard. She stopped and held out her hand—which I shook firmly—and said "How are you?"

"Pretty good," I said.

"Pretty good?" she repeated. "No, you're great!"

"Well, I guess I'm great then!" I repeated with a chuckle. After that, whenever I had the opportunity to greet Mary Kay and she asked "How are you?" I always said, "I'm great!" and I meant it.

"Is your wife a new Sales Director?" Mary Kay asked.

"Yes, she is. This is our son Kyle. I'm just tagging along with him so that she can nurse him during her breaks." I'm not sure why I felt compelled to explain all this to her, but I did.

"What is her goal?" she asked.

"She's going to be a National Sales Director," I said.

"I know that she'll do it! Just remember to always encourage her and pat her on the back — high up."

"I'll be sure to do that, Mary Kay," I said.

I smiled at her advice and she continued walking down the hall. She stopped many more times to speak to people as she made her way toward the end of the hallway and gave each person her undivided attention. Finally she stepped into the waiting elevator. The door closed, and she was gone.

The words "I know she'll do it" stayed with me until the day that prediction came true. In fact, I told that story on stage when Lisa debuted as a National Sales Director in July of 2000. I only wish Mary Kay could have been there in person to see it.

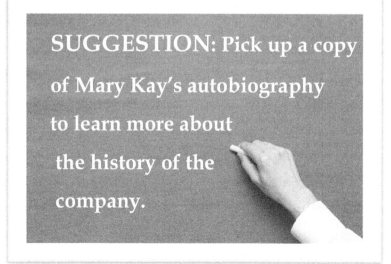

SUGGESTION: Pick up a copy of Mary Kay's autobiography to learn more about the history of the company.

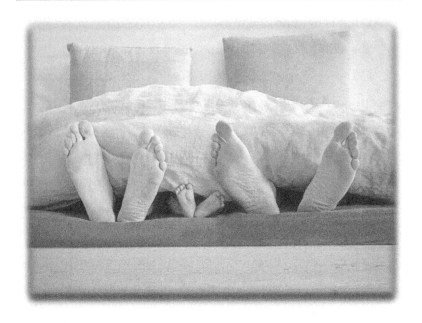

Chapter 5 KIDS

I would have been an active, involved parent whether Lisa had started a Mary Kay business or not. I was enthusiastic about our decision to have kids soon after we got married. I was an eager and willing participant in the actual production of all three kids. I was involved in all three pregnancies and present at all three deliveries, each of them memorable. I'll never forget watching my first child being born and feeling an overwhelming sense of gratitude…that I was created the man rather than the woman.

Rachel was delivered in the middle of a cold January night in 1983. Should we be blessed with a girl, we had decided, inspired by a James Taylor song, to name her Sarah Maria. When she was born, we looked at her and didn't think she looked like a Sarah Maria. She looked like a Rachel, so we changed her name to Rachel Elisabeth. She was a joyful, affectionate person from the time she was born and remains the same effusive person as an adult.

A year and a half later in November of 1984, Jonathan forced his way into the world on the eve of Ronald Reagan's second election as president of the United States. Lisa was two weeks overdue and she was huge! She knew she was huge and I knew she was huge, but I tried really hard to avoid using that word when she asked how she looked.

The labor pains began just as we sat down to enjoy a pepperoni pizza and listen to election results. From past experience and from contractions that had started to increase in frequency, Lisa knew it was time to get to the hospital. We rushed to the car, and by the time we were halfway to the hospital she was convinced that she was going to have the baby right there in the front seat. I wasn't crazy about that delivery option, so I redoubled my efforts to get her to the hospital as quickly as possible.

When we arrived, I said, "Do you want me to drop you off at the door or should I park the car and walk with you?"

"Ohhhhh, it hurts," was all she said.

I decided to park the car so that I wouldn't miss anything. Together we made it to the emergency room entrance where I explained to the nurse that my wife was about to give birth. She grabbed a wheelchair, put Lisa in it, and sped her toward the delivery room. When we got there we were told that the doctor on call had not yet arrived. The nurses were scurrying around trying to get everything ready when the doctor finally barged into the room. His glasses were askew, his hair was disheveled, and he was trying to put on a sterile pair of gloves.

"She's fully dilated and the baby is ready to come out," the nurse told him.

The doctor looked at Lisa and said, "Stop pushing! I'm not ready yet!"

"I can't stop pushing," Lisa yelled back. "The baby's coming!"

By the time the doctor finally got into position, our second child had partially emerged. After a final push, the doctor grabbed the baby, clipped the umbilical cord, and handed him to the closest nurse. Only then did we catch a glimpse of what had appeared. The baby was enormous! His head was misshapen from his express trip into the world; he was blue and covered with slime. The nurse had difficulty holding him Without help from her assistant. After seeing him and getting

34

over the initial shock, our first inclination was to name him Sasquatch.

When our vision cleared we decided to call him Jonathan. After cleaning him up, the nurse placed him on the scale. He weighed in at 11 pounds, 2 ounces and was measured at 22 1/2 inches in length. The head nurse handed the baby to Lisa and went right to the phone that was on a desk across the room. She dialed the nurses' station one floor below and said to whoever answered, "You have *got* to come up and see this baby!" Within minutes there were half a dozen other nurses crowding the delivery room staring in amazement at our enormous new baby.

Jonathan was too big to fit into the newborn diapers and T-shirts. The nurse located some larger clothing and bundled him in an extra-large blanket, and we immediately enrolled him in first grade.

> **Lisa never used our kids as an excuse not to succeed in her business. In fact, it was just the opposite. The reason she decided to become a beauty consultant in the first place was to earn extra money for Christmas presents for them in the winter of 1986.**

The third and final addition to the Madson clan made his appearance nearly four years later in March of 1988. Lisa's third pregnancy was no walk in the park. She had a terrible time with stretched stomach ligaments and a sore back and was bedridden for the entire last month. That month also happened to be her final month of qualification to become a Sales Director, but that's another story.

Kyle's birth was relatively easy, however, and it was made more enjoyable for both the doctor and me as it came right toward the end of the college basketball season. In fact, Kyle was born in the early afternoon during a great game between North Carolina and Notre Dame.

Lisa delivered our third child in the comfortable confines of a family birthing room, replete with a big color TV that hung right over the foot of her bed. The game just happened to be on. It was obvious that her doctor had delivered a lot of babies because he managed to bring Kyle into the world with both eyes glued to the TV set. It was only after the delivery that I noticed his undergraduate diploma had been earned at the University of North Carolina. To this day I still can't comprehend why Lisa had no interest in the outcome of that game.

Lisa never used our kids as an excuse not to succeed in her business. In fact, it was just the opposite. The *reason* she decided to become a Mary Kay Independent Beauty Consultant in the first place was to earn some extra money to buy Christmas presents for them in the winter of 1986.

One of the best examples that Mary Kay set for us and all the sales force was the image of a parent who worked hard for the sake of her children. She also involved her children in her business, and everybody profited.

If you were to ask our kids about the benefits of growing up in a Mary Kay family, I doubt they would remember what we got them for Christmas in 1986. But I bet they could spend hours telling you about all the other wonderful things that have happened as a result of their mother's business.

They would tell you about their trips to Seminar. When Lisa's unit was recognized as the #1 unit in all of Mary Kay each year from 1994 to 2000, our kids were there on stage every time. During that first Seminar it got so late on the evening Lisa was named Queen of Unit Sales that Kyle fell asleep in my lap. I had to wake him before we went up on stage to join his mother. He spent the rest of the night squinting into the spotlights trying to figure out what was happening. Not only did our children enjoy the excitement of being on stage with their mom; they also met other kids with whom they formed lifelong friendships.

They would tell you about the amazing trips they've been able to enjoy over the years. Spring break vacations to Hawaii. Houseboat trips to Lake of the Ozarks and Lake Powell. Trips to Florida to visit their grandparents and play golf with their friends. Now as young adults, they plead with us to bring them to Seminar each summer.

They would tell you about the educational opportunities they were afforded. Rachel spent a semester studying in Australia and had the time of her life. She met new friends from all over the country and graduated from college debt free.

They would tell you about what it was like to watch both of their parents work hard and how it felt to set big goals and achieve them. And, more importantly, what it was like to fail, get right back up, and keep going.

While Lisa was busy building her business I was busy teaching. Our kids attended the school where I taught, so I had the unusual privilege of teaching and coaching all of them. When Lisa went to her success meeting on Monday nights, or held a skin care class on Tuesday or Wednesday, or traveled out of town to work with her people, we managed to survive. I got to be a pretty good cook. Working together, the kids and I could prepare, eat, and clean up a good meal in less than 12 minutes. We could pack four lunches for the next school day in about 3 minutes. We developed routines to keep the house tidy and manage the enormous amount of laundry generated by a family of five, and we had a lot of fun.

In addition to the lessons our kids have learned over the years, there is one other aspect that bears mentioning. The company as a whole understands and respects the fact that most Consultants and Sales Directors are also wives and mothers. When Mary Kay established her priorities of God, family, and career, she meant it. She knew from personal experience that if those priorities got out of whack, nothing seemed to work right. If those priorities were honored, she knew that a family could keep balance in their lives and still achieve great things.

That point was driven home to us in a most dramatic way a couple of years after Lisa began her business. In 1995 when Lisa was the #1 Sales Director in the company, she was asked to travel to Germany to speak to the German sales force during their annual awards seminar. Six months earlier, we had learned that Kyle, our youngest child, had type 1 diabetes, an incurable disease that would affect him for the rest of his life.

The night before she was supposed to leave for Germany, Lisa was packing for her trip when she heard Kyle run to the bathroom. Concerned that his blood sugars might be high, she tested him. The meter that he used didn't even register a number. Instead it just said, "Danger! Call doctor!" She rushed into the bedroom where I was sleeping, shook me awake, and told me what had happened. "Kyle's meter said 'Danger! Call doctor!' What should I do?"

"Well, call the doctor," I said calmly.

I had to teach in the morning, so Lisa took Kyle to the

emergency room and he was admitted for further testing. She stayed with him through the night and soon realized that she was not going to be able to keep her commitment to the company. She dreaded the call she knew she would have to make in the morning.

She called the company at 8 o'clock, saying, "I'm so sorry, but I'm not going to be able to leave for Germany this afternoon. My son Kyle is in the hospital and I just can't leave him."

The woman she spoke to didn't try to make her feel guilty. Instead she said, "How are you doing? And how is Kyle? Is he going to be all right?"

The company personnel knew that Kyle needed his mother more than they did. They called a retired National Sales Director, purchased a business-class plane ticket to Germany, and sent the other woman in Lisa's place.

A few days after Kyle was released from the hospital we learned that a strep infection had caused his blood sugars to spike. Lisa made a follow-up call to the company to explain the details. It just so happened that she and I were scheduled to leave for Paris on the Top-Directors trip the next week and Lisa wanted to assure the company that it would be fine for us to go.

The travel division informed Lisa that in order to change our reservation she would have to drive to the airport, present a doctor's excuse for the change, and get a new set of tickets. The woman from Mary Kay apologized while explaining that we would have to pay the $50 transfer fee since the airline was refusing to accept the company's corporate credit card. Lisa happily obliged and took care of the requisite changes. The following week we flew to Paris. The first morning when we got up for breakfast we were met in the lobby by a member of the travel staff, who handed Lisa an envelope. Inside was a check for $50.

Lisa always says that if she were given the chance to tell one story about the value Mary Kay places on family priorities, this is the story she would tell. It would be my choice too.

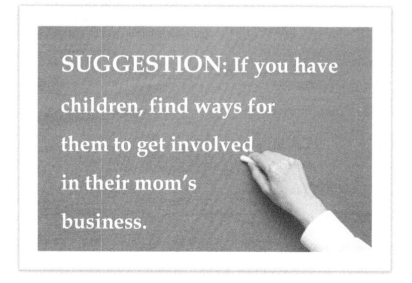

SUGGESTION: If you have children, find ways for them to get involved in their mom's business.

Chapter 6 WORK

There's no magic formula for success in any business, but I think it's fair to say that good old-fashioned hard work is one of the common factors behind most great accomplishments.

I learned a few things about work as a little boy. My dad was a pastor, my mother was a homemaker, and I had two brothers and two sisters. On Saturday mornings when we got up, my mom gave each of us a list of jobs we had to complete before we could watch cartoons or go outside and play with our friends. We cleaned toilets, washed floors, swept sidewalks, folded clothes, tidied our bedrooms, raked leaves, and so on.

During the summer we were drafted to help with the vilest of jobs — weeding our parents' vegetable garden, which took up a sizable portion of our backyard. For some reason it seemed as though I was assigned this task more frequently than the others. When I asked my mother about the apparent inequity, she said, "You work the fastest and do the best job." I'm not sure if she meant it as an honest compliment or if she was just trying to mollify one of her disgruntled workers. As much as I despised that garden, learning to pull weeds did equip me for my first real job.

We lived in southern Minnesota at the time, and most of the farmers in that area raised soybeans. They hired kids in the summer to "walk beans." Outfitted with long-sleeved shirts and wearing oversized work gloves, we walked up and down each row of those vast fields pulling out velvet-weed and other unwelcome wild plants that could break a farmer's combine if they were allowed to grow unchecked. It was hard work, but the $9 we were paid for a day's work and the delicious lunches prepared by the farmer's wife were satisfying enough to make the effort seem worthwhile. Today, when driving past fields of soybeans, I still scan them to see how well they've been walked. More than once I've been tempted to stop the car, get out, and pull a big velvet-weed that somebody missed.

Even though these jobs brought money and taught me

———

43

lessons about work, weeding my parents' vegetable plot and walking beans fueled a latent resentment toward gardening in general. When Lisa and I moved into our first small home on the east side of Madison, I immediately headed to the backyard and pulled up the railroad ties framing a small garden plot that had been maintained by the previous owner. Rachel, who was four at the time, watched me with a curious look on her face. I don't think she had ever seen me tackle a job with such passion. After I turned over soil that was still littered with rotting tomatoes and spit on the plot for good measure, she said, "Dad, why are you so mad? Don't you want to grow tomatoes in our backyard?"

"Honey," I said grimly, "if we need tomatoes or any other vegetables, I'll buy them in the produce department at the grocery store. That's why God created produce departments." Little did she realize that I was saving her from the heinous task of pulling weeds in the backyard on Saturday mornings before she could watch cartoons or go outside and play with her friends.

When I was 10 years old I lobbied my parents to allow me to get a paper route. My dad had bought used bikes for my sister and me the previous summer, and my sister's bike had cracked in half as she rode it home from the bike fixer's house, Leaving her bruised and bloodied. I rode for a year in constant dread that I might suffer the same fate and was determined to earn enough money to buy a brand-new bike.

The following year, when I was in sixth grade, my family moved to Wisconsin so my dad could serve a rural congregation outside of Madison. That summer I began working for a dairy and tobacco farmer who lived nearby. The work I did on his farm over the years helped transform me from a scrawny city kid into a strapping young adult.

Lisa grew up on a dairy farm in south central Wisconsin. As she's said about her childhood, "My dad and my older brother did most of the outside work on the farm while my mom worked in the house all day, but I watched them. When I was little, my dad occasionally asked me to help in the barn while he tested for milk quality. I spent most of my time riding my tricycle up and down the alleyway of the barn hoping I wouldn't get kicked. When I was a freshman in high school, I remember driving tractor while my dad baled hay. I put on a bathing suit and worked on my tan. I had trouble letting the clutch out slowly and flipped my dad off the back of the hay wagon more than once that day. I think that was the only time he ever yelled at me."

Even though she wasn't out helping with the chores, Lisa saw how hard her dad and brother worked. Morning and night, 365 days a year, those cows had to be milked. There were no holiday breaks and no vacations. Besides working on the farm, her dad also held down a part-time job as a rural mail carrier. "I learned that hard work doesn't hurt," Lisa has said. "My parents worked so hard, but they always had smiles on their faces. It seemed to me that hard work could actually be pleasurable."

When Lisa started her Mary Kay business, it didn't take very long for her to develop a consistent work schedule. Her Sales Director had Monday night success meetings in her home, and Lisa started attending them immediately. After her very first week of sales ($682), she came home from her meeting wearing a paper crown that made me wonder if she hadn't slipped away to the local Burger King for a birthday meal.

"Nice crown," I said when she came in the door.

"I was the Queen of Sales," she said. She was keyed up and didn't seem to notice the sarcasm in my voice. It would be the first of many crowns she wore.

As a self-employed businesswoman, Lisa was never told when to work or how hard to work. She just figured it out by herself over time. It was a process that took some adjusting on the part of both of us, but we realized the potential she had to do well in this business.

From the very beginning Lisa worked consistently, and her schedule as a Consultant became familiar to everybody in the family. On Monday nights she attended her Sales Director's success meeting. On Tuesday, Wednesday, and Thursday evenings she held skin care classes. If she had a cancellation, she would call customers or work on some other task in her elegant basement office next to the fuel tank. Fridays and Saturdays were reserved for family activities, most of which centered around football, volleyball, or basketball. On Sunday nights from 6:00 to 9:00 p.m., Lisa would make booking or coaching calls or pre-profile people who had scheduled appointments during the upcoming week.

> ## As a self-employed businesswoman, Lisa was never told when to work or how hard to work. She just figured it out by herself over time.

Every Sunday evening I sat at the kitchen table and prepared my schoolwork for the week. While I worked I couldn't help listening to Lisa on the phone. I can still remember her end of the dialogues. "Hi, Julie. This is Lisa Madson with Mary Kay. I understand that you will be attending Paula's skin care class on Wednesday night. Is this a good time for you? Do you have a few seconds to answer some questions about your skin? Great!" I gradually learned the names of her customers and the terminology she used, although to this day I still don't know what a T-zone is.

After Lisa became a Sales Director and started leading a group of her own Consultants, her schedule was similar, except that she spent more time teaching and helping others in addition to her personal selling appointments. She conducted her own success meetings on Monday nights. On Tuesday and Wednesday evenings she would travel to different areas where she had pockets of people. She would conduct meetings with her Consultants, interview prospective unit recruits, or teach a skin care class. On Thursdays she would call every single guest who had been invited to one of her meetings the previous nights. I can still hear what she said in her conversations with those guests.

"Hi, Stephanie. I'm Lisa Madson, Joan's Sales Director with Mary Kay. Do you have a quick minute? Great! I'm calling because I wanted to thank you for coming out to our event on Monday night. It meant the world to Joan, and I wanted to personally thank you. I also wanted to get feedback from you to help me become a better Sales Director. What did you like best about the meeting, and if you were in my position running the event, is there anything you would change about what I did?"

People often ask Lisa how many hours a week she works. It's difficult for her to answer that question. She never punched a clock or logged hours in a notebook. She just enjoyed what she was doing and became a firm subscriber to Mary Kay's belief that "when you love what you do, you'll never work another day in your life."

SUGGESTION: Set aside 15 minutes each Sunday night to discuss your schedules for the upcoming week.

Chapter 7 SACRIFICE

The first time I felt that Lisa's Mary Kay business was an inconvenience was in June of 1987, about eight months after Lisa signed her agreement. We played on a co-ed softball team back then and were scheduled to compete in a weekend tournament that started on Saturday morning. The night before, Lisa informed me that she was going to skip the first game on Saturday to attend a quarterly awards workshop conducted by the Sales Directors from the Madison area. I couldn't believe that she would give up playing in such an important event for that! I tried to talk her out of it, but she said, "It's important for my business for me to be there. I'm going."

Our first opponent in the tournament was the Union Cab "Huggie Bears," a team of crazies that had two cross-dressing men on their roster. Demonstrating what I thought was a misguided display of gender misidentification, both guys showed up at games wearing kilt-like skirts, lipstick, rouge, and dangly cross earrings. If they thought this might help their team circumvent the mandatory on-field ratio of five women to five men, they were mistaken. Their hairy legs and moustaches were a dead giveaway. Sadly for us, they had beaten us in a game earlier in the season, and we had a score to settle.

Later, it seemed like a good thing Lisa had decided to give up her spot on the team that day to attend her workshop. There were enough female casualties during that first game to fill a small urgent care center.

Three women suffered serious injuries during the course of that game — two from our team. "Dirty" Barb, our best female player, blew out her knee sliding into second base trying to break up a double play. The men gave the women on the team what we thought were appropriate nicknames.

51

Dirty Barb earned hers by routinely sliding into bases even though sliding was generally frowned upon in the league for two reasons—it was supposed to be a friendly, noncompetitive league, and everybody wore shorts. Barb hobbled off the field with help from her husband but refused to have the knee checked until after the game.

Then "Speedy" Linda, one of the slower women on the team, tripped over first base and broke her right wrist while trying to beat out a single. She rarely hit the ball at all, but in this instance she punched a blooper over the third baseman's head. He fumbled the ball for a couple of seconds and then dropped it. Speedy Linda was still only halfway down the line. After what seemed to me like a minute, the fielder got a handle on the ball and turned to throw. The ball sailed over the first baseman's head, and Linda cruised down the first-base line. She hit the bag, stumbled, and fell flat on her face. As her husband brushed her off and helped her off the field, he asked "What happened?"

"I was going too fast!" she cried. Unlike Dirty Barb, Speedy Linda went directly to the emergency room for X rays.

I was playing shortstop that day, despite being left-handed, because I had a pretty good arm. In the last inning a woman from the other team tried to score from second base on a ball that was hit over our left fielder's head. As the cutoff man, I angled down the third-base line and went deep into the outfield to catch the cutoff throw. As soon as I got the ball, I wheeled and threw a 200-foot, chest-high laser that would have beaten the runner home by 20 feet if she had not been directly in the path of the ball. It hit her right in the middle of the back with a sickening thud and dropped her like a stone. If it had been a foot higher, it probably would have killed her. As things turned out, she was left with a grapefruit-size welt decorated with softball stitching. To add insult to injury, our third baseman scooped up the ball and tagged her out as she lay sprawled in the dirt.

Lisa came to the next game later that afternoon, and I informed her that it was good she had missed the first game. She might have been maimed. For her part, she proudly showed me the trophy she had earned as the best overall Consultant at the workshop. For my part, I was happy to report that we had defeated the despicable Huggie Bears 10 to 3.

As Lisa's business grew we both made adjustments in our schedules. Today when I talk about the adjustments that I made, I sometimes refer to them as sacrifices; but in all truth, the decisions I made were based on logic and what would be best for our family in the long run. I knew that Lisa needed time to hold classes and do phone work, and I was willing to make sure she had that time.

In order to earn a little extra money and to satisfy my

appetite for high-energy excitement, I officiated high school basketball during the winter months and umpired high school baseball during the spring. My high school basketball coach had offered to teach us the fundamentals of reffing, and I took him up on the offer. During college and for the next seven years I gradually worked my way up the reffing ladder until I had a decent varsity schedule.

The problem was that when Lisa had a skin care class and I had to ref on the same night, we were forced to find babysitters for Rachel and Jonathan, who at five and four years of age were not quite ready to stay home by themselves — although I tried to convince Lisa that they were responsible enough to give it a shot. Even at five, Rachel had great mothering instincts.

I had an endless supply of babysitters from my seventh and eighth grade classes at school, but none of them could drive, so I had to taxi them to and from our house. We finally found an elderly lady from our church who was willing to sit with the kids at night once or twice a week. And she could drive. Even though she wasn't actually related, the kids called her "Grandma." Playing with the kids or chasing them around the house was not her style. Her preferred method of supervision was to sit in the rocking chair in the family room, watch TV, and knit. She would not allow the kids to leave that room from the time we left home until we returned a couple hours later.

This routine continued for most of the winter. One night after both of us came home, I set my paycheck on the kitchen table. The average pay for a varsity game back then was $35. I also had to buy my own gas and spend time traveling to and from games. When Lisa got home from her skin care class, I asked her how it went. "Great," she said. "I sold $370 and got two bookings and a possible recruit."

> **I knew that Lisa needed time to hold classes and do phone work, and I was willing to make sure she had that time.**

I didn't say anything at the time, but I knew what needed to be done. It was foolish for both of us to be gone at night when we had little kids at home. After assessing the situation, I made the decision to give up doing something that I enjoyed. I finished the season and then farmed out the games that I had already scheduled for the next two seasons to a buddy of mine.

With the success Lisa was having at selling and recruiting, I knew it made more sense to free her up to hold as many appointments as she could.

As a young husband, father, teacher, and coach, I didn't have a whole lot of time for recreational pursuits. Even though I lived in Wisconsin, I didn't hunt or fish. Instead I enjoyed running, reading, golfing, and doing things with my family. I coached my boys from T-ball through their teens. And we were active in our church. I discovered that with some planning and communicating, it was indeed possible to keep our priorities—God first, family second, career third—from getting out of whack.

The priorities that Mary Kay established for her company back in 1963 have been tried and tested. The mistake a lot of people make is misinterpreting the third priority on the list. When Mary Kay said career should be third, she didn't mean 23rd or 43rd. She meant third. Lisa and I managed to work hard at our careers, run a well-balanced family, and pursue recreational activities as well. At the same time, we were both willing to forego certain things in order for her to have time to focus on building her business.

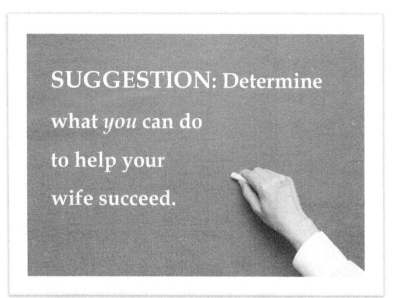

Chapter 8 SEMINAR

When I travel with Lisa I speak briefly at each of her guest events. I welcome the men in the audience and share a story that hopefully encourages them in the support of their wives. I don't think anybody will ever confuse me with Zig Ziglar or Anthony Robbins, but I do get a standing ovation at most places when I'm introduced. I'm never certain if the ovation is for my reputation as a speaker or because I'm married to Lisa. I fear the latter might be the reason. When I get on a roll, I'll elicit a few head nods in agreement with my obscure analogies and perhaps a couple of chuckles before I turn the microphone over to my wife. After each event, almost without fail, a consultant or Sales Director will approach me and ask the following question:

"I love my business and I want to do well, but I just can't get my husband on board. What can I do to get his support?"

I tell all of them the same thing. "Earn some money for him, and take him to Seminar."

If your wife is new to the company, it's possible you don't know anything about Seminar. When Lisa started her business, I certainly didn't. That's not to say I didn't research the company in my own quiet manner. For example, when Lisa received her starter kit, I pilfered the *Consultant's Guide* from underneath a pile of papers on her desk and read it cover to cover. I also found a book in her office called *There's Room at the Top*, a collection of "I Stories" featuring all the National Sales Directors at that time. I read each story and was intrigued by the varied backgrounds of the women who had made it to the top and the husbands who had helped them get there.

After Lisa held classes in November, December, and January during her first year with the company, her Sales Director suggested that she consider attending a company function in Dallas called Seminar. After supper one night Lisa said, "My Director told me it's possible that I could be on the

National Court of Sales if I keep up what I've been doing. If I achieved that, I would get to walk across the stage at Seminar in Dallas and get a beautiful ring as a prize. And she said that you have to come too."

"Now wait a minute," I said. "First off, what is this Seminar thing?"

"It's the big Mary Kay convention in Dallas each summer."

"How much will it cost?" I asked. I automatically asked that question whenever Lisa shared an idea with me.

"Don't worry about it," she said.

> **After each event, almost without fail, a consultant or Sales Director will approach me and ask the following question: "I love my business and I want to do well, but I just can't get my husband on board. What can I do to get his support?" I tell all of them the same thing. "Earn some money for him, and take him to Seminar."**

I didn't pursue the matter. As it got closer to June, the final month of the sales year, it appeared that Lisa would reach her sales goal. She told me what it would cost to attend Seminar. As a diminutive thinker back then, I thought it would be too expensive for both of us to go. I suggested that it would be better if Lisa went by herself and I stayed home with the two kids. Lisa persisted. "My Director said you *have* to go. Don't worry about the cost. I'll hold some extra classes and earn the money for both of us to go." And that's exactly what she did.

My parents agreed to watch our kids while we were gone. In early August of 1987 we packed up the Ford Tempo and headed to Minnesota. We dropped the kids off in St. Peter, proceeded to I-35, and set a straight course for Dallas, Texas.

We had reservations at the Fairmont Hotel in downtown Dallas and checked in with the rest of the people in Lisa's National Area. I still had no idea what to expect, but I was happy to be there without the kids. We attended a "Red Jacket" meeting, met some new people, and looked forward to the first day of the convention.

It's a day I'll never forget, and it changed the way I thought about Mary Kay. I suspect some of the things that impressed me might be considered silly by others. On Day 1 of Seminar we drove to the Dallas Convention Center and took the escalator from the parking garage to the main entrance.

People were streaming toward the entrance from all directions. A Dixieland band playing outside the front doors greeted the crowd while security personnel checked IDs and ushered people inside. I could feel a buzz of energy in the air as we walked into the building and were carried along with the crowd toward the breakfast hall.

I was impressed with how soon everybody was seated and

how efficiently breakfast was served. We ate quickly and headed to our seats inside the main auditorium. The opening general assembly was scheduled to begin at 8:00 a.m., and I liked the fact that at 8:00 a.m. the lights dimmed and the show began. Friends of Time, Mary Kay's dance troupe, opened the assembly with an incredible medley of singing and dancing. Then Mary Kay made her initial appearance from behind stage. The crowd erupted! I had never seen anything like it.

Lisa and I sat with her Sales Director in the upper deck to the right of the stage. Both of us were impressed by the National Sales Directors we saw for the first time — they were dynamite. Over the course of the next three days I took in all that I could. I attended a couple of the husbands' classes to hear from Dick Bartlett, president of the company at that time, Richard Rogers, and Mary Kay herself. I toured the manufacturing facility and met people from all over the country. Most importantly, I replaced the black and white snapshot of the company that I had developed inside my own mind with a full-color big picture.

On Awards Night, I watched proudly when Lisa was introduced as a member of the National Court of Sales after only nine months with the company. She waved happily to the crowd, walked across the stage, and picked up the stunning diamond ring she had earned.

During general assembly the next morning, we watched

---

video highlights of a trip the company's top Sales Directors had earned the previous year. It looked like an amazing adventure but so far out of the realm of possibility for us that I quickly dismissed it as a hopeless dream. After some of the career car drivers were introduced on stage, I leaned across Lisa's lap and said to her Director, "Do you think Lisa could ever earn a car?"

"Earn a car? She'll be a Sales Director by this time next year."

Driving to Dallas had been easy. We were well rested and excited about the new adventure. Driving home was a nightmare. After three days at the convention with very little sleep, we were exhausted. We packed the car and started home. It was 110 degrees that day and our car had no air conditioning. Our plan was to leave early Saturday afternoon and drive straight through the night until we reached my parents' home. We headed out of Dallas on I-35 with the windows down. It felt as though we were driving through a blast furnace, but neither one of us seemed to care. We were too excited about what we had seen and heard. I turned the radio off, and Lisa and I spent the next 10 hours talking about who she could call for classes, who would be good at the business, and what I could do to help.

Around midnight neither one of us could keep our eyes open. I was driving at the time. Lisa couldn't sleep because she was worried I'd run off the road. I could have slept, but I was behind the wheel. We finally pulled into a wayside thinking we could catch a few winks and then continue our journey home. I rolled down the windows in the 90-degree nighttime heat, but Lisa was convinced that wild animals or muggers — or both — would jump into the car and assault us. So I rolled up the windows and left a crack open at the top, and we tried to sleep. After 10 minutes the inside of the car was sweltering. We were both sweating, adding to the alarming travel stench that already permeated the interior of the car.

"Let's just keep going," I finally said.

"Fine," she said, "but if you start getting tired, promise you'll wake me up."

"I will," I said, but I don't remember much after that. In fact, I'm not sure who ended up driving the rest of the way.

Somehow we managed to struggle home, and we pulled into my parents' driveway the next morning dog-tired. Still, we wanted to share with somebody the exciting time we had experienced in Dallas.

At one point during Seminar, Lisa's National Sales Director had asked her about her goals in the business. "Your goals should be so big that when you tell your friends they'll laugh at you," the National said. And then she advised Lisa to tell somebody about her goals. Lisa tried out the advice immediately.

"I want to earn my first company car," she told the National.

"Say, 'I *will* earn a company car,'" was the reply. "And then set a date."

"I will be in my car by Christmas," Lisa said. I immediately started laughing.

When we got back to Minnesota, Lisa felt compelled to share her goals with somebody else. My brother was the first person to greet us when we arrived home. Lisa got out of the car and said, "Guess what, Pete? I'm going to earn a free car!"

"You are?" he said, sounding very excited.

"Yes, and I'm going to have it by Christmas."

"That sounds cool," Pete said.

The fact that Pete was only 12 at the time was irrelevant. Lisa wanted to tell her goal to somebody.

That memorable first trip to Seminar was a turning point in my support for Lisa. I had been helpful up to that time in her career, but I knew I could do more. I also understood that if she worked diligently, she could achieve many of the things I had seen in Dallas. Without saying anything to Lisa, I resolved in my own mind to do whatever it took to allow her the freedom to pursue her business goals as hard and as fast as she could.

Not only that, the events of Seminar inspired me to be a

better teacher, better husband, and better father. I heard Mary Kay and her son speak about goals and achievements, hard work and integrity. I met other couples who were great examples of what could happen when a husband and wife teamed up to support each other in their careers. My experiences at Seminar in 1987 galvanized my support for Lisa's business. We were on our way!

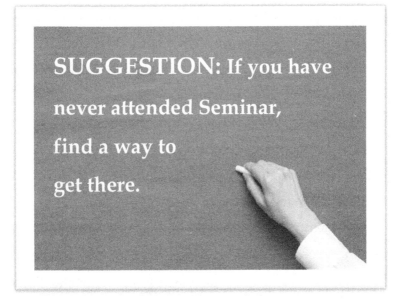

SUGGESTION: If you have never attended Seminar, find a way to get there.

Chapter 9 TRAVELS

Saying that Lisa and I had a limited travel budget when we got married is like saying that Ashlee Simpson is a bad singer — it is the epitome of understatement. Not only was our travel budget limited; so was our food budget, our clothing budget, our toiletries budget, and our entertainment budget. Actually we had no entertainment budget. Our entertainment consisted of double features at the local drive-in movie theater, and that was a splurge. We even brought our own popcorn in a brown grocery bag.

Thanks to Lisa's success with Mary Kay, our travel experiences changed dramatically. Two years after Lisa started her business and six months after she became a Sales Director, she had earned enough money for us to afford our first *international* vacation. I use the term *international* loosely, as our destination was Jamaica; our travel partners were two couples who lived on our street and had talked us into going. It was a bargain-basement trip to be sure, but we were thrilled to head off into exotic, uncharted waters.

Over the New Year's break that winter we flew coach to Jamaica from Milwaukee and were then subjected to a hellish bus ride from the airport to our resort. I use the term *resort* loosely as well. Called Club Caribbean, it consisted of a main reception/office/restaurant pavilion surrounded by a couple dozen thatch-covered shanties, many of which had suffered hurricane damage the year before and had not yet been repaired. Lisa and I shared our accommodations with an extended family of small green lizards, some of which took up residence in Lisa's empty suitcase. Despite the fact that Club Caribbean wasn't listed as a five-star resort, we had more fun than six pale-skinned Wisconsin adults should have been allowed to have.

The night we returned home, we were hit with a heavy snowstorm. I woke up the next morning to the sound of shoveling from next door. When I looked out the kitchen window, there was our neighbor shoveling his driveway. He was wearing nothing but sandals, a swimming suit, and a hat made of palm fronds that he had picked up in Jamaica. He was singing Bob Marley's "Buffalo Soldier."

> **When Lisa and I attended our first Seminar in 1987 I was enthralled by the highlight video from the Top Directors' Trip. I honestly didn't think it was something Lisa could achieve, but it sure looked like fun.**

When Lisa and I attended our first Seminar in 1987 I was enthralled by the highlight video from the Top-Directors' Trip. I honestly didn't think it was something Lisa could achieve, but it sure looked like fun. During Lisa's first years as a Sales Director, she achieved the $400,000 Unit Club and set her sights on reaching the $600,000 Unit Club the following year. If she managed to do that we would be treated to an all-expenses-paid trip to Rome, one of the most splendid cities in the world.

As a teacher and history buff, I kept my eyes and ears tuned as she worked that year. With steady persistence, a growing sales unit, and the belief she could do whatever she set her mind to, Lisa reached that goal in her second year as a Director. I could hardly believe it. That summer I petitioned the principal of my school to allow me to travel for a week during the upcoming fall. Surprisingly he agreed. I don't think either one of us realized at the time that this trip would become an annual event.

That September Lisa and I nervously prepared to join the

rest of the company's top Sales Directors on the trip to Rome. Both of us had just turned 30, and we'd be among the youngest people in the group. I stayed at school until 2:00 a.m. the night before we left, making last-minute preparations for my substitute teacher, and then went home and started packing.

Since we were going to Italy, and since I didn't have a closet full of nice clothes, my plan was to pack sparingly and buy some new clothes when we got to Rome. If I had known how expensive Italian clothing was, I would have stuffed my suitcase full of whatever I had in my closet.

The company had sent us a packet of information a month earlier that provided a lot of the details. Provided as well were luggage tags, airline tickets, and everything else we needed to make the trip enjoyable. The first leg was from Madison to Chicago. When we disembarked at O'Hare International, we felt like a couple of lost puppies. We had put our name tags on our shirts, and as we wandered into the terminal we bumped into another couple from Mary Kay, obvious veterans of foreign travel. After a quick introduction, they invited us to sit with them and have lunch, a gesture that we very much appreciated and have never forgotten.

On our trans-Atlantic flight, which was filled with Mary Kay people, I asked around to see if there were any runners in the group, hoping that I could find somebody to run with when we got to Rome. My search turned up a couple of guys who said they would be happy to have a running partner.

Above and beyond the group's remarkable friendliness and acceptance of us, a couple of incidents stand out in my memory. One occurred on the second day of our stay in Rome. On Saturday afternoon I went for a run in a beautiful park near downtown Rome. As I was returning to the hotel, I stopped to watch a pickup game of soccer being played by a bunch of kids who must have been 12 or 13. They saw me standing there in running gear and motioned for me to join them. I happily obliged and jumped right in, hoping to show off my reasonably good soccer skills. The game was taking place on a field of crushed gravel rather than grass, and I found out the hard way that it was best to remain on my feet on that unforgiving surface. My competitive dander was up, and I tried to slide tackle the ball away from one of the kids on a rush toward the goal. I slid onto my right side, scraped a large chunk of skin from my upper thigh, and left with a blazing raspberry to show for my efforts. I limped home from the park in order to attend to my wound.

The next day when I got dressed, I didn't have a bandage to cover the sore. By lunchtime my pants had been stained through with blood. When I changed clothes for dinner that night I discovered that my pants were cemented to the scab. I tried to separate the pants from the leg, but the scab stayed with the pants and the wound started bleeding again. This sorry scenario was repeated each day for the rest of the week. In the end, I did not buy any Italian clothes, and I returned home with three pairs of dress pants that had pancake-sized bloodstains on the right leg.

The other incident displayed Mary Kay's can-do attitude and uncanny ability to make the best of a bad situation. The company had planned an all-day excursion to the city of Florence for the entire group. We were scheduled to leave on buses at 5:00 in the morning for the four-hour trip north of Rome. Before we went to bed, we were reminded to notify the front desk and ask for an early wake-up call, which we did.

The next morning when I woke up there was a strange sense of lateness in the air. A midmorning light was already peeking through the heavy drapes, and I immediately grabbed my watch to check the time. It was 7:45. The hotel had neglected to call our room at 4:30. I jumped out of bed and shouted, "Lisa, we overslept! All the buses are gone!"

She bolted upright out of a sound sleep. "Are you kidding me? Call the travel desk and ask them what we should do."

I called them and explained what had happened. One of the people from Mary Kay Travel said calmly, "Get dressed as quickly as you can and meet me in the lobby in 15 minutes."

When we got downstairs she was there waiting for us. She

had called the train station and purchased tickets for us to take a high-speed train directly to Florence. She handed us a voucher for a taxi and hustled us out the door and into a waiting cab. "Take them to the train station," she told the driver.

We boarded the train shortly after 8:00 and settled in for the 55-minute trip to Florence at speeds that reached 180 miles per hour. Believe it or not, we pulled into the Florence train station just as the tour buses were disgorging the rest of the Mary Kay group after their four-hour bus trip. The rest of that day in Florence was unforgettable!

In the years since that first trip we have traveled the world, compliments of Mary Kay. After 14 Top Director Trips and five National Sales Director Trips, there are enough stories to fill a book. Suffice it to say that our appetite for travel has been sated on a regular basis, and when we travel with Mary Kay, we travel in style.

How could we forget visiting Hawaii for the first time? Or witnessing the changing of the guard at Buckingham Palace in London? Or dining with Mary Kay on the magnificent island of Bermuda? Or attending the grand opening of the Four Seasons Hotel in New York City?

How could we forget being treated to a private concert by the Vienna Boys Choir at a palace in Austria? Or riding a cable car to the top of the Matterhorn in the Swiss Alps? Or eating freshly caught salmon in Alaska?

How could we forget walking through the open-air bazaars of Istanbul? Or standing in the amphitheater in Ephesus where the Apostle Paul once preached? Or having a gondolier sing to us as he sculled us through the canals of Venice?

How could we forget visiting the Sistine Chapel in Vatican City to marvel at the works of Raphael and Michelangelo? Or staring into the haunting eyes of the Mona Lisa at the Louvre in Paris? Or sitting on a hotel balcony in Athens, a stone's throw from the Acropolis?

Mary Kay knew that many of the women in her company would also be mothers and that a mother's instinct is to give to her children before giving to herself. When she made prizes available for the members of her sales force, she referred to them as Cinderella prizes because she knew that most women wouldn't buy those things for themselves.

As a man, I appreciate those Cinderella prizes. I haven't set foot inside a jewelry store in many years. And in my opinion, the trips that Lisa and her unit have earned have been among the best ways to compensate the sales force for outstanding achievement. Those trips have spawned most of our favorite Mary Kay memories and brought us friendships that will last a lifetime.

Not too long ago, my parents made the six-hour trip from

Minnesota to Madison to visit for a couple of days. Before they left, I filled their tank with gas.

TRAVEL TIP: If you ever go to Bermuda, don't rent mopeds.

Chapter 10 DREAMS

Talk to me about dreams, and I'll regale you with stories about polar bears. I'm not kidding! I have recurring dreams about polar bears. Just last night I dreamed that I was fishing for bullheads with my little brother above the dam in the town where I grew up. There was a polar bear sitting on his haunches on the other side of the river, and he was talking to me. It was the first time in my dreams that a polar bear actually spoke.

Believe it or not, we were talking about where we were when Harmon Killebrew hit his 500th home run for the Minnesota Twins. The polar insisted he was there; I told him that *I* was there and certainly didn't see *him*. Then the polar bear started swimming across the water. His eyes were glowing red, and I wasn't sure if he was after my string of bullheads or if he meant to rend me limb from limb. Before I could find out I woke up in a cold sweat! But I digress.

I knew a lot of things about my wife before I married her. She talked a lot, which was good for me because I didn't. We held long, heartfelt conversations deep into the night and I didn't have to say a word. She liked to eat. I appreciated that because my previous girlfriend ate like a sparrow, which often made me feel like a pig. And Lisa usually wound up as the center of attention whenever we were in a group. I used to tease her about it because I thought she purposely tried to attract this attention, when in truth, people just liked to be around her. I don't tease her about it any longer. That gregarious part of her character propelled her to the top of the Mary Kay world.

On the other hand, there were a few things I learned about her *after* we were married. One, she worried a lot. She worried about mice getting into our house when the weather turned cold. I said, "Hey, mice have to live somewhere." She worried about whether the doors were locked when we left the house. I said, "If somebody needs a 20-year-old sofa, he's probably a lot more desperate than we are." She worried about whether we would have enough money at the end of the week to go out for a Friday night fish fry. I said, "What's wrong with Hamburger Helper?"

My first impulse was always to say, "Honey, don't worry about it," but that never seemed to work. Then I thought I'd try to capitalize on this quirk in her personality. I figured I could hire her out to worry for other people. Folks that had a lot on their minds could call her and tell her their problems. Lisa could add their worries to her list and free these people from their troubles. Of course, they would have to pay for the service. That innovative business plan never materialized, and when I told Lisa about it she said, "Ah, nobody would have called me anyway."

Another thing I learned about my wife after she started her Mary Kay business was that she was a dreamer. And I'm not using the term in a negative, patronizing way. Dreaming at times other than when I slept always came hard for me. I grew up in a family that lived according to the practical rules of the Puritan work ethic with a Norwegian Lutheran twist. You worked hard; you supplied yourself with the basics you needed to survive; you gave back to the Lord a portion of what He provided you. And you never took for granted the tasty hot dishes and Jell-O desserts served by the Ladies Aide at church potlucks on Sunday afternoons.

I heard Mary Kay exhort her people to 'dream big.' I never quite understood what she meant until my wife started practicing the concept. What follows is one of the most remarkable stories of Lisa's Mary Kay journey.

In September of 1987, nearly a year after she started her business, Lisa attended a small pacesetter class in her Sales Director's basement. It was for people who wanted to earn the use of a Mary Kay career car. One of the challenges given to Lisa during this class was to make an affirmation tape. An affirmation is simply a positive statement asserting that a goal the speaker or thinker wishes to achieve is already happening.

Her Director said, "Talk in the present tense about where you will be in your business next month, next year, five years from now, 10 years from now. Talk about the dreams you have and the goals you will accomplish. And sound excited!" Being the obedient Consultant that she was, when Lisa got home that afternoon she pulled out her tape recorder and completed the assignment immediately.

> **I heard Mary Kay exhort her people to "dream big." I never quite understood what she meant until my wife started practicing the concept.**

I have to tell you here that positive affirmations are a way of life for me. I never write them down or record them; I just think them in my head. Sample affirmation: *In about five seconds I will be scratching that hard-to-reach spot just under...ahhh...got it.* That's better. See? Affirmations really work!

What follows is a word-for-word transcript of the tape Lisa Made nearly 20 years ago.

"It's September of 1987 and I'm on target for my car. My friends think it's pretty exciting. I've got five recruits now and things are going pretty well. It looks as though I could do what I didn't even dream I could do when I signed up with this company.

By December 1987, I've made my car. I've got 10 recruits and we're all doing great with our production. Sue Pankow's leading the group and she's really doing well. I got a couple that like to do a little bit and then some who like to do very little that just signed up right now. But they're happy at what they're doing and that's all that matters.

They've just delivered my red Firenza. It's pretty exciting. It's exciting to see how excited all the unit is that I've been able to do this. It's also exciting to see my husband and how proud he is of me. And my parents...they kind of scowled a little bit when I said I was getting into Mary Kay and they've been very supportive as they've seen me grow in my progress. And so now that I've just got my car delivered, they're as proud as can be. Now I'm really excited and things are rolling so I'm setting my sites on Directorship.

Now it's December 1988. It's been a year of hard work and now I'm able to debut as a Director. My money is going to start doubling. We're going to have the debut at the Holidome on East Washington in Madison. Gonna have a meal and all my family and friends are there and all the Consultants...I have a singer singing really neat songs and my Director and I have to keep looking up at the ceiling because we both cry easily.

We're able to live differently...my family...we're changing the house...we're remodeling the entire house...new cupboards in the kitchen...new flooring. Got an interior decorator here changing everything. Rachel's in kindergarten now and Jonathan's in preschool and I have a new baby and I'm able to do all this and be in management in Mary Kay. And they just delivered my brand-new pink Cougar. People always teased about having a pink car but I feel very proud to be in a pink car because we know that the good ones are driving the pink cars.

Now it's 10 years later and I'm debuting as a National Director. It's really something what Mary Kay has done for my life. I'm able to carry on a good relationship with my family and not be such a hard worker that's gone from early morning 'til late at night to have a career like I do. I'm able to work it around my family and I'm able to have the priorities of God first, family second, and career third. I'll get a brand-new pink Cadillac for the rest of my life every two years. How nice.

We're building a new house...we seem to have grown out of this one. Got a brand-new gorgeous humungous house...huge pool in the backyard and a sauna. Quite the life. I think I'll keep this job.

After Lisa made her affirmation tape, she listened to it over

———

and over for the next several months before tossing it into a box in her office. It eventually was buried underneath a pile of junk and there it stayed until she came across it quite by accident in 1996.

One afternoon, as Lisa was organizing her office (not one of the tasks on her affirmation tape), she asked one of her secretaries to sort through some boxes of old tapes that had outlived their usefulness. She said, "Listen to each of them. Throw the ones that are no good, and keep the ones we might use again."

Half an hour later, her secretary said, "Lisa, you have got to listen to this tape!" She had run across the affirmation tape Lisa had made nine years earlier. Together they listened to the tape and laughed. "We laughed because nearly everything that I talked about on the tape had already come true. And we laughed at how I sounded. My Director had told us to *sound* excited. Instead of sounding excited I just used the word *excited* over and over again."

Three years later, in August of 2000, Lisa debuted as an Independent National Sales Director in Dallas. As part of her speech as the #1 Sales Director in the company that year, she played the affirmation tape that she had made 13 years earlier. Self-fulfilling prophecy? I don't know, but I do know that from the beginning of her career, she always nurtured big dreams in her heart and worked like crazy to make them come true.

I don't know what you dream about at night. My guess is that it isn't about talking polar bears with glowing red eyes that want to do you bodily harm. Hopefully you dream about more tangible things like financial independence, freedom to travel, owning your own home, college educations for your kids, and increased contributions to your church or favorite charity. Mary Kay is a business venture that can make those kinds of dreams come true.

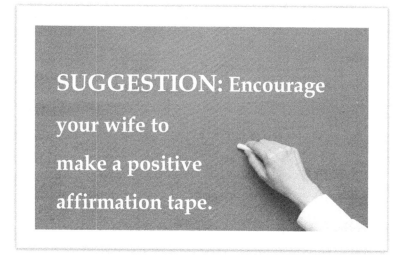

SUGGESTION: Encourage your wife to make a positive affirmation tape.

Chapter 11 MONEY

Have you ever heard somebody say "Money is the root of all evil"? That person is crazy! And he has perpetuated the untruth reflected in a common misquotation of a Bible passage. Money isn't the root of all evil. The *love* of money is the root of all evil. Money, in and of itself, is a wonderful commodity. Those pieces of paper and disks of metal that we give in exchange for a product or service can do a lot of good.

I don't think I'm going out on a limb when I say that most people could use a little more money. If you can look me in the eye and say, "I have all the money I can use," one of three things is most likely true. You recently won a $350 million Powerball jackpot, your name is Bill Gates, or you're delusional. If you have enough money to cover ALL your financial obligations, entertain yourself and your family, and scratch every possible philanthropic itch, then I have but one question for you concerning your money...*Can I please have some?*

When the Sales Director who met Lisa at the print shop sat down with her at our kitchen table to tell her about Mary Kay, she talked about the different reasons people joined the company. Those reasons included but were not limited to money, recognition, self-confidence, career cars, advancement opportunities, and being your own boss. Lisa *listened* to everything the sales director had to say but *heard* only one thing, and that was the part about the money. This was not because she was obsessed with money. It's difficult to be obsessed with money when you don't have very much.

It's not as though she didn't understand the other benefits, but recognition at that time didn't motivate Lisa. She got plenty of that from me. "Honey, the Hamburger Helper was *scrumptious* tonight!" She had plenty of self-confidence within her own circle of friends. As a former cheerleader, she was still able to do the splits 10 years after graduating from high school, a claim that none of her friends could make. Thoughts of earning a car, promoting herself before she had even started, or being her own boss were ideas completely foreign to her at the time. She was interested in one thing—earning a little extra money for our family.

We were by no means destitute at that time in our lives, but like a lot of young couples with kids, we struggled to make ends meet. Thinking about our investment portfolio didn't keep us awake at night. We had no portfolio. Our cash reserve would have enabled us to buy, hmmm…let me think, absolutely nothing. We were trying to get by on my meager teacher's salary and the two or three part-time jobs Lisa held, including her job as a cashier at a farm implement store, owing to which she earned $70 a week, wore a blue smock with *Vicki* embroidered on the front, and smelled like tires when she got home. During her conversation with the Sales Director from up the street, one thought kept running through her mind. *If I could earn $70 a week selling Mary Kay, I could quit my job at the farm store.*

Before Lisa started her Mary Kay business, we did a reasonably good job of managing what we had. And we were happy. I grew up in a family that didn't have a lot of money, but none of us lacked anything. My parents were careful and resourceful and I don't ever remember wishing I had things that other kids had. Well, except for the snowmobiles that my friend Byron had. And the in-ground pool that my friend Todd across the street had. And the concrete basketball court that my other friend Tim up the street had. Except for those things, I was pretty happy. Whenever I suggested to my dad that I thought we could use a snowmobile, a swimming pool, or a basketball court, he just laughed at me.

When I wanted something that my parents couldn't afford to buy, I learned that there was a simple solution. Find somebody that would pay me to work for him or her, earn the money, and buy it myself. I never had much difficulty finding work. As a kid I walked beans, delivered papers, and shoveled snow for the neighbors. When I was in junior high and high school I worked on a farm during the summer months and during the school year whenever I had time. During my years in college I washed dishes at a restaurant, officiated grade school basketball games, packed onion rings, cleaned the meat department at a grocery store, and milked cows for Lisa's dad.

From the time I was a little kid, I understood and appreciated the value of money. I realized that it was hard to get and easy to lose. Still, one of the simplest and most memorable lessons I learned about money was taught to me by my Legion baseball coach when I was 17. During the summer after my senior year in high school my summer baseball team was warming up before a doubleheader. Our coach was a character who spouted inspirational sayings at every opportunity. Before one game he walked into the dugout where a bunch of us had congregated. He noticed a penny lying in the dirt, picked it up, rubbed it clean, and put it in his pocket. A couple of us saw him do it, and one kid said, "Hey, Coach, whatcha gonna buy with that penny?" I'll never forget the answer.

"If you aren't careful with little things, you'll never be trusted with big things," he said. We won that game, and for the rest of the summer we joked around with our coach by placing a penny somewhere conspicuous in the dugout before each game to see if he would find it. It turned into a pregame ritual and a bit of a good-luck tradition. Every time he saw the penny, he picked it up, brushed it off, and put it in his pocket. We won a lot of games that summer.

I will readily admit to anybody who asks that there were only two things that got me excited about the business opportunity Lisa was about to pursue — the money and the car. Why? We *needed* more money and we *needed* an extra car. I wasn't too concerned about the other so-called benefits. Before Lisa actually started holding appointments that first week in November of 1986, I will also admit that I was a little dubious about the whole scenario. I had unpacked her inventory and hoped she'd actually be able to sell it.

Lisa had been told by her Sales Director to book some skin Care classes with friends and/or relatives, so she did. She practiced her presentation on me and my brother at the kitchen table one afternoon while we watched a football game

> **I think it's safe to say that most women start Mary Kay businesses with the main goal of earning some extra money. After all, that's what businesses are for. Most husbands are interested in the same thing.**

on the TV across the room. We sat there like test-market guinea pigs with hair clips on our heads and stuff all over our faces, but I don't think we paid very close attention to what Lisa was trying to do. A few days later she sat me down for a second practice session. She went through her entire skin care class presentation, reading from her flip chart and sounding like a Mary Kay robot. At the end, I said, "Would you like my advice?"

"What?" she said.

"Just be yourself and have fun," I told her.

On November 2, 1986, she finally headed out the door for her first appointment. It went very well. So did the next one, and the next one, and the next one, and the next one.

At the end of the week when she tallied up her sales, she informed me that she had earned $682. You might wonder how I could remember that figure after 20 years. It's easy. That was an enormous amount of money for us back then.

Lisa kept 40% of that as clear profit. She put 50% of her

sales back into her inventory and used 10% of her sales for gifts for the women who held classes for her. Still, the 40% profit she cleared from her first week of sales made a statement to me.

The tepid support I had given Lisa up to that point suddenly became very enthusiastic. I started doing some quick calculations in my head. *If she could sell $682 every week ,in a month that could be...and in a year that could be...Whoopeeeee!* Little did I know that my calculations would eventually come out on the *low* end.

The next week I said, "Hey, Lisa, how many skin care classes do you have scheduled for the week? Do you need any extra help with anything?" From that point onward in her business, I was completely on board.

I think it's safe to say that most women start Mary Kay businesses with the main goal of earning some extra money. After all, that's what businesses are for. Most husbands are interested in the same thing. The fact that Lisa has earned a lot of money in her career is not lost on me. However, the other benefits that Lisa's Sales Director told her about bear mentioning again.

Recognition: This book has a whole chapter on this one, but here I'll just point to Lisa's discovery that recognition was important to her. In fact, I believe it was one of the driving forces behind her success.

Self-confidence: Even though Lisa could still do the splits 10 years after graduating from high school, she shook like a leaf at her first skin care class. She was so nervous that she broke out in hives. Gradually, however, she became more and more comfortable speaking in front of people. Today she speaks regularly in front of thousands of women (and men) all over the country.

Career cars: The first car that Lisa earned, the red Olds Firenza, has an interesting story. After Lisa earned her pink Cadillac, her father bought the Firenza and used it as a second car for 17 years. When he finally traded it in for a different vehicle, it had been driven for well over 100,000 miles. Lisa is awaiting the delivery of her 10th pink Cadillac as I write this.

Advancement opportunities: There was little hope for Lisa to advance in any of her previous jobs. Where could she have been promoted when she worked as a sales clerk in the children's department of a retail store? To the women's department? Where could she have been promoted when she typed reports for a rural appraiser? To actually doing the appraisals? Where could she have been promoted when she cashiered at the farm implement store? To head the tool department?

Lisa started out like every other woman in Mary Kay, as a brand new beauty consultant. If she wanted to climb the career ladder designed by the company, it was completely up to her. There was no time frame; there was nobody behind her pushing her out of the way and nobody above her trying to squelch her ambition. Each time she advanced in the company it was her decision.

Being your own boss: In all fairness, the appraiser that Lisa worked for was a wonderful boss. He allowed her great flexibility, especially when it came to our children. He praised Lisa for her good work and was generous with her pay. A couple of years after Lisa had quit working for him and started to build her own business, they were talking after church one Sunday. Her old boss said, "You know, Lisa, you were the best secretary I ever had."

Lisa said, "You know, you were the best boss I ever had — until I started working for myself!"

In addition to those great benefits came flexibility, great friends, new skills, travel opportunities, and many others. I'd like to think that one of the reasons that Lisa and I have been blessed through her business in a big way is that we were careful with the little things. For that I say, "Thanks, Coach!"

SUGGESTION: Study and learn about the Mary Kay marketing plan and the company's Ladder of Success.

Chapter 12 BALANCE

I think the Baby Boomer generation of parents, to which we belong, screwed up. I'm not quite sure how it happened, but somehow we allowed ourselves to become overworked, overindulgent, overextended, over permissive, overinvolved parents. Most of us work full-time jobs and try to raise children all the while struggling to resist the relentless media onslaught that seeks to convince us that we need the biggest, best, and most beautiful of everything.

I don't remember my parents looking frenzied and spent all the time. I suppose they worried about us the way we worry about our children, but our little lives were not the hub around which all family activities centered. When my dad got irritated with us for something trivial, like asking for a ride to school when we just as easily could walk, he'd give us lectures that always began, "When I was your age..."

"When I was your age," he would say, "I used to walk to school every day, seven miles uphill both ways, barefoot in the snow."

"Yeah, right, Dad."

If we started begging for Christmas presents before we had even eaten Thanksgiving turkey he would say, "When I was your age I had six brothers and sisters, for Pete's sake. For Christmas all we got was an orange in a brown paper sack. *If* we were well behaved. If not, all we got was a lump of coal."

"OK, Dad, but things are different today, you know."

I used to try the same strategy with my kids when I got irritated. "You know, kids, when I was..." But before I could finish, the kids interrupted me—"Dad, don't even start with the stories about when you were a kid. Things are different today."

Still, I can't help thinking back to what it was like to be a kid 35 years ago. Once school let out for the summer, we were pretty much on our own for three glorious months. My parents loved me and I'm pretty sure most of my friends' parents loved them, except for Randy Harrelson's dad, who was an ornery drunk and didn't care where Randy went or what he did. But they didn't monitor our play or pick sides for us when we played tackle football in the neighbor's backyard. They didn't drive us to the swimming pool every afternoon. They didn't arrange carpools to take us to Little League practice or games. And they certainly didn't sit in the stands and scream at the coaches and the umpires. If a kid wasn't any good, he got stuck in right field and he and his parents kept their mouths shut.

> **God first, family second, career third. In that order things seem to work. With communication, cooperation and teamwork, a balanced life can be a reality.**

We would get up every morning, get dressed, eat a bowl of Wheaties, and head out for the day. Occasionally we'd check in if we needed food or if we had sustained some sort of injury that might warrant attention from an adult. Otherwise, we'd come back home when it was time for supper, wolf down some more food, and then return to the neighborhood games that went on until well after dark. My brother and I bathed once a week on Saturday nights after my mom took us out on the back steps and gave us our weekly buzz cut. We watched Lawrence Welk (wonnaful, wonnaful) on TV and went to bed.

Things have changed, and I know it's not easy to maintain balance in a family these days. Both parents work. Kids are involved in a multitude of activities that are organized and supervised by — who else? — parents. Add a business like Mary Kay to the mix, and things become even more challenging. The good news that I can share with you is this: It is possible to find balance in your lives if you really want to. Lisa and I managed to do it, and we know a lot of other people who did as well.

When Lisa's business started to take off, we were right in the middle of the busiest time of our lives. My teaching job was very demanding. Our kids were involved in year-round sports programs. In order to maintain domestic balance (i.e., sanity and/or happiness), we gradually developed four principles that helped. I will explain them here, and you're welcome to use them or modify them to fit your own household.

I refer to the first principle as the *Sunday Night After I Do My Schoolwork and You Finish Making Phone Calls We Can Sit Down and Discuss Our Schedules for the Upcoming Week After Which I'll Make a Big Batch of Buttered Popcorn and When We Get the Kids to Bed We'll Have a Glass of Wine and*

Watch a Movie rule.

Each of us had a calendar that was penciled so full of activities that it was difficult to see the days of the week. We found that a short Sunday night planning session was an effective way to make sure we had all our bases covered for the upcoming week. I told Lisa about my school schedule and the kids' sports schedules. She told me where she was traveling and what other events she had to attend. If we needed sitters, we made arrangements for the entire week. Sometimes we had to negotiate. "If I don't have to come to your career breakfast planning session to help you set up tables on Saturday morning, I won't insist that you come to school to watch Kyle practice the part of the donkey in the Christmas pageant." After Lisa became a National Sales Director and I retired from teaching, we still held Sunday night sessions. These days they're shorter because our schedules are virtually identical. There is still the occasional negotiation, however, and it's always followed by popcorn and a movie.

I called the second principle the *I Will Do Anything Around the House EXCEPT Change the Sheets on the Bed and I Don't Care if Your Mom Used to Wash Your Sheets Every Week When You Were a Kid When I'm Ready for Bed if You're Gone and the Sheets are Still in the Dryer I'm Sleeping on the Mattress Pad* rule.

If you are a husband and father in a two-career family, I suspect you are used to helping with some of your family's household chores. It was different when I was a kid. Since my mom didn't work outside the home, she took care of most of the household tasks, with the help of her obstinate adolescent conscripts, of course. Occasionally Dad would give Mom a break by doing the dishes and cleaning up the kitchen.

When Lisa's schedule started getting busier, there were jobs around the house that always needed to be done — dishes, laundry, cooking, and so on. None of these tasks are particularly difficult, and since I was a quick and efficient worker trained by a ruthless Saturday morning list maker, I just pitched in wherever and whenever help was needed. Honestly, though, I drew the line when it came to putting clean sheets on the bed. It was my belief that sheets should be washed no more than once every six months. If Lisa thought they should be washed more frequently, I figured she could put them back on the bed. I'm dead serious in telling you that I went to sleep on the mattress pad more than once when Lisa was traveling.

The third principle we lived by was called the *If We're Out of Milk and You Happen to be Driving by the Grocery Store Why Don't You Stop In and Buy it Yourself Instead of Calling Me in the Middle of Basketball Practice and Asking Me to Pick it Up on the Way Home From School and While You're there Pick Up a Loaf of Bread and Some Bananas* rule.

The point of this principle was that when something needed to be done and one of us was not available, the other person would do it. This applied to things like picking up dry cleaning or kids, preparing a meal, or making a doctor's appointment for one of the children. If Lisa was traveling out of town, I took care of everything. If I had a coaching clinic or a weekend basketball tournament, she did the same.

If there was something that neither one of us had the time or the desire to do, we paid somebody else to do it for us. At first, this came hard for me. When Lisa wanted to hire a house cleaner, I stubbornly resisted. I thought two healthy adults with three healthy children ought to be able to clean their own home. Finally, spurred by my wife's insistence and by Mary Kay's own adage that you shouldn't spend dollar time on penny jobs, I relented and we hired somebody to clean our house once a week. That day has become my favorite day of the week!

When Lisa wanted to hire someone to help in her office, again I resisted. She was thinking about the future; I was worried about the cost. In the end, it turned out to be one of the best business decisions she could have made.

I refer to the fourth principle as the *One of the Reasons We Had Kids in the First Place Was so that They Could Help Out With Work Around the House so if Either of the Boys Gives*

You Any Lip about Mowing the Lawn Kindly Remind Them That I Brought Them into the World and I'll Take Them Out of It rule.

As parents, we were not taskmasters by any stretch, but we expected our kids to pull their weight around the house. They took turns mowing the lawn, washing dishes, folding clothes, and so on. They didn't always like it, but then, what kids do?

God first, family second, career third. In that order things seem to work.

With communication, cooperation, and teamwork, a balanced life can be a reality.

SUGGESTION: Schedule regular family time during your week.

Chapter 13 RETIREMENT

Lisa and I went to the same college to be trained as teachers. She lasted one year. Something about ancient Western civilization not making any sense and how it wasn't fair that she got a D on a midterm test and I got a B+ after she studied at the library for 16 hours and I read *Sports Illustrated* all night. Ironically, she still ended up as a teacher. It's just that her students were women instead of second graders sitting at small desks.

Whereas the idea of becoming a teacher had been planted

in Lisa's mind when she was a young girl, I didn't make the decision to attend college and pursue a career in education until I was a senior in high school. Before that I had all sorts of ideas — delusions of grandeur, some might say. When I was a kid I figured I'd play first base for the Minnesota Twins *and* be a running back for the Vikings. I also thought about becoming a doctor or a lawyer or even combining all four careers. Baseball in the spring and summer, football in the fall, surgery and litigation during the off-season.

By the time I was halfway through my senior year, I had no idea what I should do. At one point I even considered joining the military. Even though the thought of boot camp was unappetizing, the images of crisp uniforms, spit-shined shoes, and well-made beds appealed to my sense of order and neatness.

> **Lisa's success with Mary Kay had given me options that not too many guys my age could claim. I was free to pursue my love for writing, my aspiration to compete in the sport of triathlon and my desire to travel. Believe it or not, I also found time to help out in Lisa's office.**

Eventually Lisa and I, who started dating about this time, both decided to go into education. We enrolled at a small teacher training college in New Ulm, Minnesota, where I could prolong my days of playing football, basketball, and baseball and she could perfect her splits on the cheerleading squad. Her vision of life as a school teacher was nipped in the bud by a supercilious professor whose obscure ramblings about Thucydides made her question whether anybody should be subjected to the educational process. After Lisa quit school, I stayed the course through my sophomore year before transferring to the University of Wisconsin in Whitewater to finish my degree in education.

We got married after my junior year in college. Lisa had a full-time secretarial job that sustained us until I could land a teaching job. When I graduated in 1982, teaching jobs in Wisconsin were hard to find. Over half the potential educators who graduated from my class never found work as teachers. Luckily I did. I was hired to teach and coach seventh and eighth graders at Holy Cross Lutheran School in Madison. I spent 21 years there and can count on one hand the number of days that I got up in the morning and didn't feel like going to school. One of those days occurred during my first year of teaching.

I brought my seventh graders to a nearby park for physical education. It was late fall and the weather was beautiful, so I let the kids stay at the park for an extra half-hour. When we got back to school the principal was waiting for us in the hallway with a scowl on his face. It wasn't the first time I had been face-to-face with an angry principal. In fact, this had happened frequently when I was a student. It never dawned on me that it might happen when I was a member of the faculty! Suddenly I knew why I was in trouble. My class was supposed to have been back at school by 2:30 to sing for a group of elderly church members who had come to school for a special program. "Can I talk you after you dismiss your class?" the principal said.

"Sure," I said. The thought of running out the door and never returning crossed my mind, and then I gained my composure. I hesitate to admit it now, but after a stern reproof from the principal I actually started crying. He patted me on the back and told me that I should be more responsible in the future.

Meanwhile, after just a couple of months in business, Lisa realized that she could make more money with Mary Kay than with all her part-time jobs combined. She quit them one by one, determined to make this business her full-time career. She was happy, and you know what they say. "When the woman in the house is happy, *everybody's* happy." She was excited about what she had been able to do after such a short time, and she was starting to make good money. As you might guess, that made me happy.

We gradually settled into a routine. The kids and I would head off to school every day while Lisa worked in her office, held appointments, and worked with her growing sales unit. We were both happy with our careers, and thoughts of leaving the teaching profession before the normal age of retirement never entered my mind.

Over the years I got to know a lot of other Mary Kay husbands, and they came from all walks of life. There were teachers, firefighters, architects, real estate agents, and businessmen of all types. I discovered that some husbands had retired from their careers to work alongside their wives. To be honest, I thought they were crazy. The thought of working with my wife in her business never occurred to me. Two reasons: First, I enjoyed teaching and coaching. Second, my wife and I have very different work styles, and I thought we might have some compatibility issues.

I am what some people call an "ordered thinker." My kids say I'm anal retentive. I prefer to think of myself as focused. If you can answer yes to any of the following questions, you probably think like me. When eating, do you divide your food into distinct groups and then consume the groups at an even rate so that your last bite of turkey corresponds with your last bit of stuffing, your last bite of potatoes, and your last bite of cranberry sauce? While driving down the highway, do you ever find yourself tapping your foot at the point when you feel you are exactly between two telephone poles? Do you find yourself clearing dishes off the table and wiping the counters even before the kids have finished eating? I think you get the picture.

When I work, I like to tackle one job at a time. I like my work space to be free of clutter, and I like it to be relatively quiet. My wife is just the opposite. She bounces from one task to another. When an idea pops into her head, she acts on it, and it doesn't matter if there are three or four unfinished jobs on the docket. Her desk is a mess of unopened mail, notes, and lists, and her office is a cacophony of ringing phones, music, and loud voices.

After my 20th year of teaching, however, something changed. Our youngest son had graduated from eighth grade, and for the first time in 17 years I found myself driving to school in the mornings by myself while the kids were off to high school and college. It was lonely. Lisa had become a National Sales Director two years earlier and was making a great income. In October of that year, it dawned on me that if I wanted to, I could retire from teaching and pursue other things that interested me. I thought about it for a couple of days, and one night after soccer practice I came home and had a short conversation with Lisa. I said, "Honey, I think I'm going to retire from teaching at the end of the year."

"OK," she said. That was it! I finalized the decision with my principal, had a great year, and was able to retire while the kids and parents at the school still liked me. Lisa's success with Mary Kay had given me options that not too many guys my age could claim. I was free to pursue my love for writing, my aspiration to compete in the sport of triathlon, and my desire to travel. Believe it or not, I also found time to help out in Lisa's office.

While I was teaching, I was not privy to what went on in her office on a daily basis. Quite often, when I asked questions about her business, she would say, "You have no idea how much we do in this office." She was right. I had no idea until I was able to see it firsthand. By the time I left my teaching position, she had two full-time assistants and two or three part-time helpers. Our kids worked for her when she needed extra help, and I had to admit to her one day that I was impressed with the well-oiled machine that her office had become.

Our work styles do clash occasionally, but I've found ways to avoid conflict. First, I get up early and do things in Lisa's office before she or her assistants arrive. When I'm working at something and she asks me to do something else and then again something else, I calmly remind her that I need to finish one job before starting the next. And if you were to see both of our work spaces, it would not be difficult to tell which is mine and which is hers.

When people ask me what I do for a living I say, "I'm a retired school teacher and coach."

Some will look at me funny and say, "But you're too young to retire."

To which I answer, "No, I'm not." When questioned further, I'm always happy to explain the situation. "Well, you see, my wife is a National Sales Director with Mary Kay Cosmetics and…"

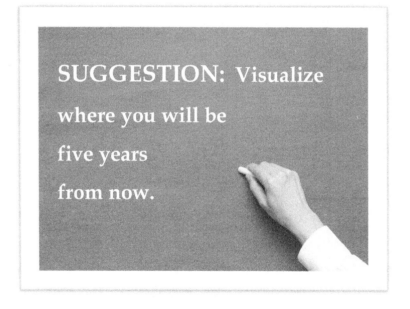

SUGGESTION: Visualize where you will be five years from now.

Chapter 14 RECOGNITION

Mary Kay used to say that there are two things people want even more than sex and money. Those two things are praise and recognition. I'm not sure if she was talking about men, but since most of the people in her sales force were and still are women, I guess it really doesn't matter. What I do know is that her liberal use of praise and recognition made my life easier.

When Lisa began her career with Mary Kay, as I said earlier, her main goal was to earn extra money for our family. I know for a fact that she was not interested in the other benefits she was told about—least of all, praise and recognition. Yet, after a short time in the business, Lisa came to appreciate and enjoy that benefit as much as anything else. When she came home from her Monday night success meetings she was usually so excited that I would have to tie her to a chair to get her to sit still and tell me about it. "I was the Queen of Sales," she told me one night. "My Director brought me up in front of the room and everybody gave me a standing ovation."

One night she came home really fired up. I asked her what happened. "I earned a red Mary Kay pencil!" she said excitedly.

"A pencil?" I said.

"Yes," she said. "A pencil! Everybody that had a $300 week got a pencil."

"Wow! A whole pencil. That's pretty exciting." I said.

"And if we have a $1,000 week we get to sit at the head table at the meeting *and* we get special recognition in the unit newsletter."

Lisa worked hard for that weekly dose of praise and recognition. She also became good at handing it out to the women who were in her sales unit. When she became a Sales Director I chuckled as she told me she was going to start giving away red Mary Kay pencils for $300 weeks at her success meetings. But when she came home on Monday nights after her meetings and told me how many women had earned that small prize and the measure of praise that went with it, I knew she was on to something. Years later, Consultants still come up to her and reminisce about how important those red pencils were to them. Many kept them as souvenirs and symbols of their early successes.

Mary Kay knew what she was doing when she based her entire marketing plan on praise and recognition. She encouraged generous applause for the successes achieved by her Consultants and Sales Directors. She made a concentrated effort to give as much recognition as possible at company functions like Seminar. Today, thousands of women work hard all year for the chance to walk across the stage at Seminar to the applause of their peers. My wife sometimes jokes that a Mary Kay gathering is the only place where a person can sneeze and get a standing ovation.

Mary Kay also knew that it was important for Consultants to see their names in print, so she encouraged Sales Directors to send out newsletters filled with the names of people who had achieved some goal during the month. I used to help Lisa with this monthly task. I went through stacks of her newsletters and highlighted the names of consultants to whom each copy was sent. I complained once in a while, but Lisa insisted that it was important, and she was right.

If asked, I would tell you that praise and recognition are

not that important to me. I will admit, however, that when my wife receives praise and recognition from the company or from her peers, I usually feel pretty good. More often than not, some of that praise and recognition is deflected my way.

Let me explain how Mary Kay's philosophy has helped me in my personal life. Lisa doesn't take the time to read a whole lot, but every once in a while she comes home with some self-help book that is supposed to enhance personal relationships. She'll set it on her desk or on the kitchen table or on the nightstand in our bedroom and read sections of it when she has time. More often than not she'll suggest that I read it too. If I decline the offer, which I usually do at first, she lets me know in no uncertain terms that if I don't read the book I will be responsible for the slow and steady decline of our relationship. In other words, the books are required reading, and I've read them all—*Men Are from Mars; Women Are from Venus* by John Gray; *His Needs, Her Needs* by Willard F. Harley, Jr.; and my all-time favorite, *The Five Love Languages* by Gary Chapman.

I mention this book last because it is the one that has caused me some consternation. If this book is not on your required reading list, allow me to give you a brief synopsis. The author contends that each person gives and receives love in one or more of five specific ways called *love languages.*

These are giving gifts, spending quality time, performing

acts of service, physical touch, and words of affirmation. Ideally, a husband and wife should try to discover which language or languages his or her partner most appreciates and then speak that language frequently. What I have discovered is that the love language that my wife most appreciates is the one that I'm the poorest at speaking. Same goes for her.

Example: For the longest time I had the mistaken notion that performing acts of service was the best way to show my wife appreciation, and since it's the love language that I speak best I speak it often. I'm always happy to tear around and run errands that are a pain in the neck for her to do. Or I'm quick to do something around the house that needs to be done. After performing these acts of service, I usually feel self-satisfied and happy that I've been able to do something for her. Time and time again it has been made clear to me that a tidy kitchen or a clean car or an empty laundry bin doesn't mean a darned thing to her. All she wants is to be told that she looks good. She doesn't care if the lawn is trimmed perfectly or if the chairs around the dining room table are spaced exactly the same distance apart or if I do all the grocery shopping. She wants to be told that her new jeans make her look thin. "Honey, do these jeans make me look fat?"

"You look thin as a rail."

"Are you just saying that to make me feel good?"

"Yes. I mean, no! I mean, yes! I mean, you look great in those jeans!"

> **If asked, I would tell you that praise and recognition are not that important to me. I will admit, however, that when my wife receives praise and recognition from the company or from her peers, I usually feel pretty good. More often than not, some of that praise and recognition is deflected my way.**

I've traveled with Lisa all over the country as she does workshops and guest events. She changes her workshop each year, but her guest event has remained pretty much the same. She tells her "I Story" and presents the marketing plan of the company in a way that is down-to-earth, easy to understand, and funny. I've heard it so many times that if something were to happen in the middle of her talk, I could step right in and finish it word for word. After each event she usually asks me the same question: "How did I do tonight?"

One night I made the mistake of offering what I thought was constructive criticism. "Have you ever thought about varying your guest event? You know, just for your own satisfaction and enjoyment?" I might just as well have suggested that she light herself on fire and jump off the

Golden Gate Bridge.

"People like my story the way it is and it's effective. I'm not going to fix something that isn't broken. Every time I tell my story lots of people sign up with the company. They relate to my story and how I tell it."

"I agree. I just thought you might want to make some adjustments to your delivery or…"

"I don't know why you can't just tell me that you thought I did a good job and that you enjoyed it. Did you ever hear Mary Kay say that you should always sandwich criticism between two layers of praise?"

"Yes! You did a great job and I *did* enjoy it. I just know that for myself I would get some creative satisfaction from trying something new once in a while."

"You're not the one speaking."

I believe the day will come when I fully understand how to speak Lisa's love language. Until that day, I will still occasionally take her wallet out of her purse, arrange her money so all the bills face the same direction, and get no thanks of any kind.

SUGGESTION: Tell your wife she looks good today or that you're proud of her or both.

Chapter 15 QUOTES

When you listen to people in the Mary Kay world speak, you will frequently hear them quote Mary Kay Ash. I'm sure Mary Kay wouldn't mind. She always encouraged her people to share ideas with each other. Some of the quotes attributed to her might sound clichéd, but they remain purposeful and meaningful.

In this chapter, I will share some Mary Kay-isms and explain how they were relevant to us.

"A woman with a man behind her is a woman and a half." Mary Kay started her company in 1963, a time when many women didn't work outside the home. It was undoubtedly a difficult transition for some husbands to see their wives pursue a business venture that would take them out of the home. Even though most women work outside the home today, support from a spouse is not always a given. When Lisa decided to join the company in 1986, I was not terribly enthused. My lack of excitement, however, was directly proportional to my lack of information and knowledge. Once I learned more about what the company had to offer and what my wife could accomplish, I became very supportive.

Over the years Lisa has discovered that if a woman is determined to be successful in Mary Kay, she can overcome a lot of obstacles. However, the one obstacle that has derailed more capable consultants than any other obstacle has been an unsupportive spouse.

Today, there are a lot of women who would like to work and still stay at home and be with their children. Mary Kay is a business opportunity that makes that possible.

"It's not where you start, it's where you finish." Truer words could not be spoken about the Mary Kay opportunity for the simple reason that everybody starts in exactly the same place. It's not possible to plunk down some money and buy a directorship. You can't skip rungs on the Ladder of Success.

Each consultant begins her business with a beauty showcase and a dream and works from there. The top people in the company, the National Sales Directors, all followed the same career path, just at different speeds. There are no timelines for an individual's success, no territories, and no ceilings. Any beauty consultant who follows the company's marketing plan can go as far and as fast as she desires.

> **Over the years Lisa has discovered that if a woman is determined to be successful in Mary Kay, she can overcome a lot of obstacles. However, the one obstacle that has derailed more capable consultants than any other obstacle has been an unsupportive spouse.**

"The speed of the leader is the speed of the gang." Mary Kay realized that one of the best ways to motivate others to success was by succeeding herself. When Lisa became a Sales Director she still held regular selling appointments and continued to build her personal team. Leading by example is the best way to help others succeed in Mary Kay.

"You fail forward to success." When Mary Kay's company became successful, some people thought the achievement came easy to her. She always offered to show those people her knees. She knew hers would be the bloodiest. What great success story hasn't come on the heels of many failures? Not

many. After finally finding a way to keep a light bulb filament burning, Thomas Edison said, "I didn't fail; I just found 10,000 ways that didn't work." Every success story in Mary Kay is fraught with moments of failure. Those failures often become the best teachers. The women who persevered and succeeded in spite of their failures can testify to that.

"Aerodynamically the bumblebee shouldn't be able to fly, but the bumblebee doesn't know that so it goes on flying anyway." The bumblebee is the symbol of success against all odds that Mary Kay adopted. When Mary Kay wanted to start her business she was told by others that it would never work. The odds stacked against her were too great, and her chances of success were minuscule. Mary Kay flew in the face of conventional wisdom, tackled the long odds, and became a great success anyway. The same can be said for thousands of women around the world who made the decision to become successful right along with her.

"No matter how busy you are, you must take time to make the other person feel important." This characteristic defined Mary Kay's personality. It all stemmed from an experience she had with a superior at a company for which she worked. While speaking to the president of that company one day, she noticed that he kept looking past her to see how long the line behind her was. Mary Kay never forgot how that made her feel. There were countless times when she was surrounded by

hundreds of women, yet she always gave her complete attention to the person to whom she was speaking. She always chided her sales force to imagine that each person they spoke to had a sign around her neck that said, "Make me feel important."

"If you think you can, you can. If you think you can't, you're right." Your attitude controls your life. With a business like Mary Kay it is paramount to understand how closely related a great attitude is to your success. Every woman in Mary Kay has to deal with forces, both internal and external, that conspire to keep her from succeeding. Simply put, a good attitude will allow a positive reaction to every situation you encounter. If you think you can, you can.

"Sandwich every bit of criticism between two thick layers of praise." Mary Kay believed in praising people to success. She didn't mean empty praise for a job poorly done, but sound praise for worthy achievement. One of my wife's strongest attributes is her ability to recognize and reward achievements by her people. There are certainly times when constructive criticism is called for, even necessary; but being quick to praise and slow to criticize is an idea to live by. This is a lesson that I fear comes hard to many husbands. If it is heeded, however, the results can be amazing.

"If it is to be, it's up to me." My wife calls Mary Kay a self-improvement course that you get paid to take. From the time

she signed her agreement, Lisa implemented a self-imposed responsibility to do things that would allow her to succeed. Some of them were personal in nature while others were focused on business. To this day, she continually strives to be a better leader and learn new ways to motivate her people, implement technology, and teach others what she has already learned.

"When you come to a roadblock, take a detour." Sounds easy, but it's not. A person's true character is not revealed when things are going well but when things are *not* going well. Every woman in Mary Kay encounters obstacles that block her road to success. The women that succeed are the ones that find a way to go over, above, around, or through those obstacles.

"If you love what you do, you'll never work another day in your life." My wife uses this quote frequently. Why? Because she believes it and *lives* it every day of her life. In a recent survey of American workers, when asked if they love what they do for a living, 75% of them said no. Lisa has always viewed her career as a tremendous blessing. She loves going to work each day. She cherishes the position of leadership that she's earned and loves nothing more than helping other women achieve things they never thought possible. The best way to understand this quote is to realize that my wife hasn't worked in 33 years.

SUGGESTION: Display some inspirational quotes in your wife's office.

CONCLUSION

When Lisa started her career with Mary Kay, there was no handbook for husbands. Had there been such a thing, I would have read it. Even though I was skeptical at first, I was curious about what my wife had gotten herself into. Consequently, I made the effort to find out what Mary Kay Cosmetics was all about. I read her *Consultant's Guide* from cover to cover. I perused *There's Room at the Top*, a book that featured all the National Sales Directors in the company at the time. Each month I looked through *Applause* magazine, the company's recognition publication. I always turned to the section where the company listed the commissions earned by its top people. I could hardly believe what they were making. My thought was, "If one person can do it, so can somebody else. And if somebody else can do it, why not Lisa?"

More importantly, I kept my eyes and ears open. I listened to Lisa when she talked on the phone. I watched her as she went about her business. I kept an open mind about what she could achieve, and I never made her feel guilty for working hard and striving to be the best. And, last but not least, I decided that I was going to get involved in her goals and dreams and do whatever I could to help her.

Over the years, I learned a lot from my wife. I learned about *integrity* as I watched her to do things the way Mary Kay wanted. I learned about *conflict resolution* as I saw her address issues that arose with people in her sales unit. I learned about *attitude* as I watched her keep going after being disappointed by classes that cancelled or by prospective Consultants that changed their minds at the last minute.

Today when a husband asks me what I did to help Lisa in her career, I can honestly tell him that I did a little bit of everything. I don't try to take credit for Lisa's success, but looking back, I realize now that my contributions were significant. The most important thing I did was to give her the freedom to do whatever she needed to do to become successful. The freedom that I gave her has now returned to me.

*E*pilogue

It's been 14 years since I wrote *A Woman with a Man Beside Her*. A lot has transpired since then!

Lisa's Mary Kay business has continued to grow. When Lisa debuted as an Independent National Sales Director back in 2000, her role as a leader changed. Most of her time since then has been spent building new leaders in the Madson National Area. Her very first recruit in the business, Sue Pankow, became a National Sales Director in 2014 and between them they lead National Areas that total more than 100 Sales Directors across the country.

During this past Seminar year, Lisa was recognized as the #3 National Sales Director nationwide and the #1 National Sales Director in the Diamond Seminar. Her total career earnings to date exceed $14 million dollars.

When Lisa was thinking about joining the company back in 1986, she had called Sue, a former beauty consultant, to ask her advice. Sue said, "Don't do it! There's no money to be made in Mary Kay!" Lisa jokes with Sue to this day about that advice and is often heard to say, "If I had listened to her, we'd both be broke today!"

In addition to a couple of my own business ventures over the past 20 years, I've spent much of my time involved with my wife's business. We travel the country together to work with her Independent Sales Directors and beauty consultants. We've been all over the world on amazing company trips. We've developed lifelong friendships with many other Mary Kay leaders and their families.

Our family has grown as well. When Lisa started her business in 1986 we had two small kids, ages three and two. A third was born in 1988, the year Lisa became a Sales Directors. All three kids are married now and between them we have six beautiful grandchildren. Lisa's original goal when starting her business was to earn $70 a week so she could quit her job as a cashier at the farm store and still afford to buy Christmas presents for the kids. Creating memories for her entire family still motivates and inspires her every day!

It's been a memorable journey for both of us. Mary Kay used to say that a woman with a man behind her is a woman and a half. I'd like to think my contributions to Lisa's success reflect Mary Kay's vision for both of us!

Made in the USA
Monee, IL
13 June 2020